D1563042

Children of Divorce

Children of Divorce

A Practical Guide for Parents,
Attorneys, and Therapists

WILLIAM BERNET, M.D.

Medical Director
The Psychiatric Hospital at Vanderbilt

Associate Clinical Professor in the Department of Psychiatry
Vanderbilt University, Nashville, Tennessee

VANTAGE PRESS
New York

The following publishers have granted permission to reprint their material:

Bulletin of the American Academy of Psychiatry and the Law, excerpt from W. Bernet, "The Noncustodial Parent and Medical Treatment." *21:* 357–364, 1993.

Journal of the American Academy of Child and Adolescent Psychiatry, excerpt from W. Bernet, "The Therapist's Role in Child Custody Disputes." *22:* 180–183, 1983.

Krieger Publishing Company, Malabar, Florida, excerpt from J. E. Meeks and W. Bernet, *The Fragile Alliance,* 1990.

FIRST EDITION

Copyright © 1995 by William Bernet

Published by Vantage Press, Inc.
516 West 34th Street, New York, New York 10001

Manufactured in the United States of America
ISBN: 0-533-11373-3

Library of Congress Catalog Card No.: 94-90820

0 9 8 7 6 5 4 3 2 1

Contents

Acknowledgments

This book became a family project. My wife, Susan, encouraged me through many drafts and revisions. My children and stepchildren—Henry, Alice, Daniel, and Elizabeth—provided some of the examples used in the book. My mother, Florence Bernet, proofread the manuscript.

Several colleagues and friends—Linda Wirth, LCSW, William Mitchell, M.D., Barry Nurcombe, M.D., and William Licamele, M.D.—read earlier versions of *Children of Divorce* and made helpful suggestions. Psychotherapists learn most of what they know from their clients and patients, so I am very thankful to the children of divorce whom I had the opportunity to meet over the last twenty years. Several secretaries, including Karen Williams, Debbie Frahm, and Cheryl King, have been helpful and supportive.

Introduction

There is a need for this kind of book. There are already many books about parenting that cover every period of life from infancy to the stage of adult children still living at home. There are many books for individuals who are getting divorced, that help people deal with their feelings of anger and loss and loneliness. There are professional books for therapists who might be treating divorced individuals and their children. There is not very much available for divorced parents who are trying hard to raise their children. Raising the children of divorce is a challenging task. For many divorced parents, raising their children comes on top of having a full-time job and trying to reestablish social relationships.

This book is intended for several audiences. It is primarily intended for parents who are divorcing or are already divorced and are hoping to raise their children in a healthy manner. This book is also intended for legal professionals, both attorneys and judges, since they help shape the lives of the children of divorce. I think attorneys and judges will find some of my suggestions to be unusual, but innovative and useful. This book is also intended for therapists and school personnel who work with children of divorced families. Although it is not a technical treatise, this book does have many ideas that therapists, counselors, and teachers should find helpful.

This book is about two big issues: *conflict* and what to do about it; *stability* and how to provide it as much as possible. My underlying premise is that children of divorce are injured by the lack of stability in their lives, but especially by the continuing conflict between their parents. This book does not dwell on the problems, but emphasizes solutions. It offers many ways to minimize the conflict that children of divorce experience day in and day out. Many of the suggestions in this book are very easy to bring about and could be implemented independently by either the custodial or the noncustodial parent. Some of the suggestions are more complicated and require the active cooperation of both parents. A few of them, such as suggestions in the chapter about "Uncommon Custody Arrangements," might require attorneys and the action of a judge.

Getting divorced is not a rose garden. The divorce presumably came about as a way to resolve difficulties between the couple, but it creates a whole new set of issues. In particular, it creates the problem of helping the mother and father, who now dislike each other very much, find ways to cooperate in raising the children. There are no easy answers. Simplistic solutions are not usually much help, because each divorced family has its own particular nuances and requirements. I will present, however, important general principles and many specific suggestions that divorced parents should find usable and practical.

The ideas in this book have been derived from many sources, including my personal experience with a blended family and conversations with friends and colleagues who have been divorced. My clinical work as a child psychiatrist has allowed me to meet and treat many children of divorce and their parents. As a forensic psychiatrist, I have met children and parents and attorneys and judges when I was asked to do custody evaluations. Case material is sometimes mentioned in this book. At all times, of course, names and other details have been changed to protect the individual's and the family's confidentiality.

I have attempted to make this book gender neutral. For example, sometimes the custodial parent is referred to as "he" and sometimes as "she." Likewise, the child in one example might be referred to as "he" and in another example as "she."

Children of Divorce

Chapter One
Basic Strategies

Then there came two women that were harlots, to the king, and stood before him; and one of them said: I beseech thee, my lord, I and this woman dwelt in one house, and I was delivered of a child with her in the chamber. And the third day, after that I was delivered, she also was delivered, and we were together, and no other person with us in the house, only we two. And this woman's child died in the night, for in her sleep she overlaid him. And rising in the dead time of the night, she took my child from my side, while I thy handmaid was asleep, and laid it in her bosom, and laid her dead child in my bosom. And when I rose in the morning to give my child suck, behold it was dead, but considering him more diligently when it was clear day, I found that it was not mine which I bore. And the other woman answered: It is not so as thou sayest, but thy child is dead, and mine is alive. On the contrary she said: Thou liest, for my child liveth, and thy child is dead. And in this manner they strove before the king.

Then said the king: The one saith: My child is alive, and thy child is dead. And the other answereth: Nay, but thy child is dead, and mine liveth. The king therefore said: Bring me a sword. And when they had brought a sword before the king: Divide, said he, the living child in two, and give half to the one, and half to the other. But the woman whose child was alive, said to the king (for her bowels were moved upon her child): I beseech thee, my lord, give her the child alive, and do not kill it. But the other said: Let it be neither mine nor thine, but divide it. The king answered, and said: Give the living child to this woman, and let it not be killed, for she is the mother thereof.

And all Israel heard the judgment which the king had judged, and they feared the king, seeing that the wisdom of God was in him to do judgment.

1 Kings 3:16–28

1

The timeless story about Solomon from the First Book of Kings contains messages that are meaningful for divorced parents and their children. The basic plot is being reenacted hundreds and thousands of times in every city: it is the story of two adults disputing their right to a child; the dilemma of the judge attempting to determine which adult is truly more worthy to take the child; and the baby, who is being destroyed in the process. Another motif is the woman—presumably the true mother—who was trying to balance her own right to the baby with the baby's right to stay in one piece and survive the custody dispute. In the story of Solomon, the true mother decided that the baby's right to life was stronger than her own right to possess the baby.

Parents and judges should not take the story of Solomon completely literally. Today, however, Solomon's order to cut the baby in half may be a metaphor for court-ordered joint custody. The outcome looks the same in that neither parent is really pleased with the court's decision and the child suffers. Also, it may be that the parent who is willing to give up some control, by ensuring that the child maintain a good relationship with the other parent, is the preferred custodial parent.

It is hard to imagine how much suffering is experienced by the children of divorced parents. It starts during the marriage itself, when the child is aware of the disagreements and fighting between the parents. When one parent angrily packs up and moves out of the family home, the child may be confused and frightened. A child may experience a time of disbelief, when she knows in her mind that her parents are splitting up, but does not accept it in her heart. Her suffering continues after the divorce, as she is whipsawed from one household to another and from one relationship to another.

Since the process of separation and divorce will not disappear at any time in the foreseeable future, there is no way to completely protect our children from the consequences. But it should be possible to identify the major causes of distress for the children of divorce and to minimize their impact. Every family situation will have its own idiosyncrasies. However, we can devise some general guidelines for parents who are divorcing, which are intended to minimize the pain and the damage to the children. The basic principles for raising children of divorce are explained in this chapter. These principles form the foundation for the rest of this book. These principles are easy to explain, but parents may find them hard to follow. Subsequent chapters in this book will provide specific methods for minimizing the suffering of the children of divorce. There is no way to remove it completely, but it should be possible to lighten the burden of these children.

There are three basic principles that are important for divorced parents to know and remember. This book will relate practical suggestions for ways to implement these principles.

1. Children of divorce should have a good relationship with both parents.

It is not always possible to achieve this goal. Sometimes the circumstances of life prevent a child from knowing or enjoying both of his parents. One or both of the parents may have died, abandoned the child, been abusive, or sustained a chronic illness that required the parent and the child to be apart from each other. In most divorces, however, there are two parents who should be able to develop and maintain a healthy, mutually satisfying relationship with the child. The biggest factor that prevents a child from having a good relationship with both parents is the amount of arguing and fighting between the parents.

There are many aspects of parental separation and divorce that pain the children. The long list of potential hurts includes the sense of uncertainty and insecurity because the family is not going to be together the way it used to be; the embarrassment when friends find out about the parents' divorce; the prospect of moving several times before the custodial parent settles down again; the daily and weekly disruptions to everyday life as the child shuttles from one household to the other; the loss of the noncustodial parent as he or she drifts further out of one's life; and the inevitable financial hardships, because it costs more for divorced families to live in two households than it did for the intact family to live together.

Of all the things that hurt when parents divorce, the part that aches the most is the fighting. Divorced parents fight in every which way. They fight *over the children,* in custody disputes that go on for years. The fight *through the children,* by using the children as the carriers of parental vindictiveness. And they fight *in front of the children,* especially when the children are passing from one household to the other at the beginning and end of visitation. By the way, divorced parents do not have a monopoly on fighting in front of the children. Angry displays between parents are also damaging to the children of intact families.

3

This book does not have very many statistics, but here are a few. Approximately one-half of all marriages in the United States end in divorce. That means that about half of all children will spend some time in a single-parent household. Since half of the divorces occur before the seventh year of marriage, there are many divorced parents with young children. Each year over one million children experience the divorce of their parents. If you happen to want more statistics, refer to "Children and Divorce" in *The Future of Children,* Volume 4, published by the Center for the Future of Children, the David and Lucille Packard Foundation, 1994.

If divorcing parents were willing to hear and accept one piece of advice, it should be, "Don't fight with your former spouse." Of course, that is an extremely hard piece of advice to take. It is a suggestion that divorced parents always agree is absolutely correct, but the problem is that the *other parent* always picks the fight. If parents were able to hear and accept this one piece of advice, the children would stand a much better chance of having a happy and satisfying relationship with both the mother and the father.

The fact is that two individuals who once were in love are not going to give each other up without a certain amount of fighting. If they really did care about each other when they were together, they are bound to experience anger and frustration and resentment when they split up. What really matters, of course, is to not include the children in the fighting. If you have some serious bones to pick with the former partner, do it when the kids are in school, and try not to make your children into weapons of mass destruction. These topics are discussed in chapter two, "Fighting and the Children."

2. Divorced parents should find ways to minimize the disruptions and make life as normal as possible for their children.

Even children in normal, intact families can become stressed by the confusing, frantic schedules that they follow before school, during school, after school, and in the evening. Our busy, harried children maintain calendars that are more complex than those of many adults, such as businessmen who travel. During the course of a week, children must deal with multiple teachers, car pools, bus drivers, and a variety of athletic, musical, and religious extracurricular activities. If both parents work, the children's lives become more complicated because they spend part of the day in child-care programs before and after school and they may experience a parade of other caretakers such as baby-sitters and grandparents.

If the parents are divorced, the scheduling process can get out of control. The divorced parents may find it convenient for themselves to make different day-care and baby-sitting arrangements. As a result, that part of the child's life does not have a sense of continuity to it. If the child lives part of the week in one home and part in another, he may never completely unpack and unwind before moving in. Can you imagine what happens to a child's sense of identity and wholeness when his mother takes him to art class and to the Church of Christ Sunday school on her weekends, but the father has him on a baseball team and attending Catholic religious education on his weekends? It is not a happy experience.

The solution is for divorced parents to put some thought into how to help the child carry on with his own life in a way that is consistent and that is minimally disrupted by the needs of the parents. Making life reasonably routine and normal for these children requires several ingredients. It means, for instance, that the parents should communicate regarding the most important household rules and policies, in order for discipline to be fairly consistent in the two homes. It means that the parents should try to agree on matters such as the child's participation in organized sports teams, the child's medical care, and his religious upbringing. It means that the divorced parents should agree on details such as the celebration of major holidays, so that the child is not expected to sit through two Thanksgiving dinners on the same afternoon.

This book contains many suggestions for ways to normalize the lives of the children of divorce. The chapters that pertain to that issue most directly are chapter seven, "Living in Two Homes"; chapter eight, "Making Visitation Work"; chapter nine, "Holidays"; and chapter ten, "Noncustodial Parents."

3. Divorced parents and their children need to accept the inevitable losses and disappointments and to move on with their lives.

There are many "necessary losses" that both children and parents must accept when divorce occurs. For instance, the children will have to give up the notion that their parents will get back together again and it will be one happy family. That is a common idea that children express, even after one or both parents have married again. The children need to give up the old homestead and community and be prepared to move to new surroundings. To some extent, the children will need to give up the fullness of the relationship that they had enjoyed with both parents. Even when the divorce goes smoothly, the children are not going to have the same intimacy and the same wealth of shared experiences with the non-custodial parent.

The divorcing parents also need to acknowledge and accept important losses. Divorced parents usually have to manage on a tighter budget than when they were married. They have to give up the conveniences of a two-income household and a two-parent family. Perhaps the hardest task is to give up the relationship with the former spouse. For some reason, even couples who have grown apart and presumably cannot stand each other still have the energy to fuss and fight and stay involved with each other. It is the sooner the better, that both former spouses realize that they should not count on each other any more for moral support, for baby-sitting, for sewing on buttons, for changing the oil in the car, and for sparring partners.

Finally, it is a sad task for divorcing parents to give up some aspect of the relationship with the child. The custodial parent has to get used to the notion of giving up total authority and control over the child, by encouraging the noncustodial parent to have successful visitations and to take over the parenting of the child during those times. The noncustodial parent, of course, must give up living with the child on a day-to-day basis. The noncustodial parent needs to accept that he or she is performing with a handicap, but still plays a good game.

This idea, that divorced parents and their children need to accept certain inevitable disappointments, will come up at many points in this book. It will be particularly important in chapter five, ''Balancing the Needs of Parents and Children''; chapter six, ''Trying to Love Both Parents''; and chapter fifteen, ''Letting Go and Moving On.''

In this book we will be looking at many ideas, suggestions, and solutions. None of these ideas is perfect. Some of these ideas won't work if the other parent is absolutely and totally unreasonable. In most divorced families, both parents have contributed to the dispute. It is fortunate that in most divorced families both parents have some interest in doing what is best for the children and are looking for solutions.

A basic assumption in this book is that it is important for the children to have a good relationship with both parents. It is more important for the child to have a good relationship with both parents than it is to have an ideal relationship with one parent and a lousy relationship with the other. The implication of this assumption is that compromise will be required. If you don't believe in this assumption, the suggestions and ideas in this book will not make much sense to you.

Chapter Two
Fighting and the Children

In 1986 Robert Butterworth was campaigning for an important office, to become the attorney general of Florida. He was about to be elected. However, he and his ex-wife were also engaged in a custody dispute. On the eve of the election, his ex-wife shot their sixteen-year-old son four times, called the police, and then shot herself.

In 1993 a man in Maryland went to pick up his four-year-old daughter for visitation. However, he got into an argument with his ex-wife and with her boyfriend. The father said that he had a present in his car for the girl. He left the house and went out to the car, but returned with a long box that contained a pump-action shotgun. The man killed his ex-wife; shot the boyfriend as he ran out the door; and then shot himself. When police arrived, they found the four-year-old standing in the doorway.

Parents who are divorcing hurt their children in many ways. What hurts the most is *not* that the parents have left each other and now live in separate households and the children go back and forth. It is *not* the embarrassment that occurs when friends find out that your parents have split up. What hurts the most is the fighting that the children experience. Most of the time, the fighting of divorced parents is not as dramatic and not so brutal as the two stories at the beginning of this chapter, which were taken from newspaper reports from Florida and Maryland. In most cases the fighting does not erupt into a sudden shoot-out, but drags on through months and years of painful arguing and bickering.

Divorcing parents involve their children in three methods of fighting: they fight over the children; they fight through the children; and they fight in front of the children. *Fighting over the children* refers to the formal custody dispute, which is conducted in the local court house, and also to many informal contests, such as the competition to provide the most appreciated birthday present. *Fighting through the children* means one parent's use of the child as a weapon against the other parent. For example, the mother despises her former in-laws, so she withholds visitation because the child "has a fever" on the one weekend they are in town for a visit. The meaning of *fighting in front of the children* is more obvious. It usually happens when the noncustodial parent arrives to pick up the child for visitation.

Official Method of Fighting

In the United States, the official method of fighting is the custody dispute. American customs and legal practices have evolved together to create this expensive and painful and sometimes tragic ritual. It is sad to watch two concerned and dedicated parents exhausting both their energy and their financial resources while fighting over who is the better parent.

The basic custody dispute involves a familiar cast of characters: two parents who both feel deeply wronged by each other and whose self-esteem is now derived from the role of parent rather than the role of spouse; two attorneys who usually are sincere and well-intentioned and highly partial to the interests of their respective clients; a judge, who has heard these same accusations and counteraccusations many times; the witnesses, various relatives and friends of the parents, who are remarkably one-sided in what they remember about the family; sometimes teachers, nannies, and baby-sitters; perhaps a few expert witnesses, such as psychologists and psychiatrists, who try to bring their knowledge and experience to bear on the heavy questions before the court; and—almost overlooked as they wait at home or in courthouse hallways—the children.

The expense of this exercise can be enormous in both economic and psychological terms. Consider the financial outlay. The cost of a one-week custody battle in court—including the preparation time billed by two sets of attorneys, the transportation and expenses of various witnesses, and time lost from work—can exceed the annual cost of sending the child to this country's fanciest private college.

The emotional cost of a custody dispute can also be enormous. Both parents gear up to identify and attack every vulnerability of the former spouse. This includes exposing in a public trial the most personal and intimate facts—for example, that the mother is retarded and the father can't figure out why he married her in the first place; that the father is

9

brain-damaged after a tragic automobile accident and has difficulty tying his shoes; that one of the parents is homosexual and wrote a rather juicy letter to a lover. In other words, both parents gear up to do exactly what the child needs the least, which is to criticize and insult each other and to undermine each other's parenting roles. The emotional cost of the custody dispute is shared among the parents and the children, not to mention the various friends and relatives who have become involved in the process.

Attorneys

It is said that there are three types of attorneys:

- Type One: the pushy, powerful, aggressive attorneys, known as bombers.
- Type Two: the less aggressive, but basically competent and conscientious attorneys.
- Type Three: the wimpy, ineffectual attorneys.

Each of the three groups contains both men and women attorneys. Numerically, most attorneys who practice family law are Type Twos. There are fewer Type Ones, but they may be better known in the community because they are flamboyant and highly visible. There are only a few Type Threes, because ineffective divorce attorneys are likely to find another line of work.

The fairest and the most sensible legal battles occur when two of the Type Two attorneys are up against each other. Both of them do a good job. They do what they can to present their clients in a good light. They fight hard, but they fight clean. Also, they usually do not lose sight of the fact that the underlying purpose of the custody dispute is to determine what is in the best interests of the children.

It may also seem like a fair fight when each parent has a vigorous, aggressive Type One attorney, but it is more likely to be a brawl. Type One attorneys may go out of their way to offend or humiliate the other attorney's client; to attack and insult the opposition's witnesses; and to pursue almost any obscure technicality in order to win his or her case. They stir up so much dirt that the children and their interests are lost in a cloud of dust.

Two famous custody disputes have been related to Hollywood. *Kramer vs. Kramer* was a popular movie in 1979 that featured Dustin Hoffman and Meryl Streep. When the mother in the movie left the home and dropped out of sight, the father had to rely on his own devices to raise their son, Billy Kramer. The father took Billy to school, cooked his meals, and tried to hold down a job. After being gone for eighteen months, the mother came to realize that she wanted to be a parent again. She wanted custody of Billy. The parents went to court to resolve the dispute of Kramer vs. Kramer. If you missed the movie, you can find out what happened by placing a special order at your local video store.

In 1993 the unmarried Woody Allen and Mia Farrow waged a bitter and turbulent battle over their three children, Moses, Dylan, and Satchel. The media focused on Mr. Allen's romantic relationship with Ms. Farrow's older (adopted) child, Soon-Yi, which most people found extremely inappropriate. There were accusations that Mr. Allen had sexually abused Dylan. It was painful for the average person to read about this custody trial in the daily papers, so it must have been a nightmare for the participants. It certainly illustrates how children are the victims when their parents fight each other.

It is not a fair fight when a more aggressive attorney (a Type One or Type Two) is up against an ineffective attorney (a Type Three). What happens then is that the aggressive attorney browbeats the weak attorney and his client. The more powerful attorney is much more likely to win, but it may not seem like a just outcome because the victory is based on the lawyer's pushiness rather than on the merits of the case.

My suggestion to divorcing parents is to work with a Type Two attorney. There are many competent, industrious, and ethical attorneys in every city, so it usually is not hard to locate one who seems right. Attorneys know their colleagues in the community, so you can start your search by checking with a lawyer you may have met at work or in some other legal situation. Tell him or her that you want a solid, capable attorney—not a bomber, not a wimp—and ask for recommendations.

Since divorce is so common, you can ask friends about their experiences with attorneys. Ask specific questions that would help in your decision. Did your friend's attorney seem knowledgeable, efficient, smart, well organized? Was the attorney effective in reaching a resolution or did the case drag on forever? Did the attorney seem strong and assertive, but not vicious? Did your friend ultimately get what he or she wanted, since that is the purpose of hiring an attorney? Perhaps most important, did the attorney take the time and take an interest in listening to the client's point of view?

Judges

Compared to attorneys, judges appear to come from a more uniform mold. It is true that judges have their own personalities and styles. Some like to dwell on details, while others insist on sticking to the big issues. Some seem talkative and friendly and even humorous, while others are persistently solemn. Some are extremely authoritarian, while others take on a fatherly role toward the divorcing couple and a grandfatherly role toward the children. Despite these superficial differences, it is striking that almost all judges look and act like they are trying to be fair. They seem interested in what every witness brings to the proceedings. What is most important, they are concerned about the children. Although judges accept that it is rarely possible to devise the perfect solution for the children of divorce, they try hard to determine the best alternative of those available.

Sometimes judges do make odd decisions. For instance, one judge could not make up his mind regarding the custody of a three-year-old girl. After a lengthy hearing, he ruled that the parents should have joint custody and that the child should alternate between the two households, spending one week at a time at each location. That, in itself, is not a particularly unusual arrangement for a preschool child. The schedule of alternating weeks would not be so bad if a young child had a good relationship with both parents, if the parents lived in the same community, and if the child had the same baby-sitter in both households and was enrolled in a consistent nursery school.

The problem in this case was that the parents lived in two different communities in two different states, about an hour apart. Since both parents worked, they both had to put the girl in a local day-care program. Since they lived so far apart, the parents had to enroll her in two different day-care centers and hire two different baby-sitters. Unfortunately, these parents could not even agree on what kind of hairdo the child should have. As she passed from one household to the other, both parents would change her physical appearance to suit their own tastes. This little girl had no sense of continuity in her world, as she shuttled between her two lives. The judge had created a custody arrangement that confused and burdened the child.

Everybody is entitled to his or her own personality traits and idiosyncrasies, including judges. It does create a problem, however, when judges use their position to impose their personal opinions on other people. Occasionally there will be a judge who has very strong beliefs regarding moral issues, child rearing, or sexual behaviors. The judge may feel that a particular issue is so important—for example, "young children need a mother more than a father" or "all families should go to church twice a week"—that he does not consider all the pros and cons of the case.

Alternatives

It is not required that divorcing parents hire extremely expensive attorneys and then fight it out in court. There are alternatives. In some divorces the parents simply have a heart-to-heart discussion and decide between themselves how to deal with both financial and custody issues. They ask two attorneys to draw the agreement up in legal language, present it to a judge and that's all there is to it.

Some individuals make use of divorce mediation. In divorce mediation, a neutral professional, usually an attorney, helps the divorcing couple negotiate an agreement. For many people, divorce mediation is a great alternative to an adversarial legal dispute. Mediation is discussed in chapter fourteen.

Unofficial Fighting

The officially recognized manner of fighting over children, the custody dispute, does not last forever. It usually involves the family for several months of preparation time and several days of intense stress, but then it is over. Some divorced parents, who wish to continue to battle on their own for an indefinite duration, find many unofficial and unregulated methods of fighting.

How bad can it get, this fighting between two individuals who loved each other at one time? In its most extreme form, the fighting between ex-spouses leads to murder and suicide. That happens often enough that it no longer seems surprising to read in the newspaper about an angry divorced parent who kills his ex-spouse, perhaps kills the children, and perhaps kills himself.

Aside from murder and suicide, the fighting between divorced individuals may take many forms. The more fighting there is, the more the children are victimized. Here are several examples of fighting over the child, through the child, and in front of the child.

- The easiest way to use the child as a weapon is to infuriate the other parent by manipulating the visitation arrangements. For instance, the custodial parent repeatedly says that the child can't go anywhere on the weekend because of illness. This ploy may go on for months. Or imagine the frustration in the noncustodial parent who has driven for five hours to pick up the child for the weekend, only to find the house empty, locked up tight, and nobody in sight.
- The noncustodial parent can just as easily misuse the visitation. The child may be returned two hours late because "we ran out of gas." The child may be returned hungry, dirty, or angry, just to annoy the custodial parent.
- Parents and other relatives may abuse the child through active indoctrination. For example, maternal grandparents instructed a girl to memorize the statements, "My stepmother is a whore. My stepmother is a prostitute and will go to Hell." After learning those sentences, she was instructed to recite them when she stayed with her father and stepmother.
- Some parents fight each other by making spurious allegations of sexual abuse. They may indoctrinate the child or coerce the child to make statements describing the abuse. Of course, actual sexual abuse can be damaging both physically and psychologically. It is also damaging to put the child in the position of making allegations that are false.
- An interesting form of fighting through the child occurs when each parent claims to be doing what is absolutely best for the child. Sometimes it take the form of religious instruction. The custodial parent may have the child enrolled in Sunday school at the Catholic parish church. The noncustodial parent, however, takes the child to Jewish services every other weekend and also has him studying Hebrew. So if the child ends up confused and resentful, who is to blame? Each parent has

14

the legal right to raise the child in his or her own religion, but does it really make sense to insist on exercising that right?

● Another issue that puts the child in the middle of parental conflict is the child's appearance. Both parents may have strong opinions about what the child should wear and what kind of haircut he should have. Imagine how much anger is aroused when the mother wants her son to have long hair and the father brings the boy home with a crew cut.

● Many parents use financial issues as a rationalization for fighting in a way that involves the children. Perhaps the most common is the custodial parent who withholds visitation because the noncustodial parent failed to pay child support. Likewise, an affluent noncustodial parent may withhold money unless he gets his way in certain areas.

● Even after the custody dispute is over, divorced parents may continue to fight it out in court. A custodial parent who is passive-aggressive may force the noncustodial parent to file a lawsuit every time he wants something that should have been accomplished through routine negotiation.

● "Unofficial fighting" may seem almost bizarre to outside observers. There was a woman on "Court TV" who had presented her case, that the father had said bad things about her to their child. After the trial the woman was interviewed for the television audience and she repeated how horrible the father had been to badmouth her to the child, and she insisted that she had never said a bad thing about the father. But there she was on national television criticizing the father's parenting abilities!

In all these scenarios, the child is caught in the middle, which may cause her to have psychological problems or may lead to the development of innovative coping skills. For example, the child who is caught between two fighting parents may discover how to be diplomatic every day in every way. That is, she finds that it works best to agree with the mother when she is with her and to agree with the father when she is with him. In order to avoid being caught in the middle, some children gravitate to being completely allied with one parent or the other. In other words, they become overly attached and identified with one parent (usually the custodial parent) and alienated from the other parent (usually the noncustodial parent). This phenomenon is discussed in chapter six, "Trying to Love Both Parents."

Solutions

The fighting and the consequent emotional trauma to the children of divorce are neither desirable nor necessary. There are many possible solutions.

• Both parents should understand that the children will be better off if they continue to have a good relationship with both the mother and the father. Both parents need to accept that and to work toward that goal. That is easier said than done, but many divorcing parents are able to set aside their grievances and work together on behalf of the children. For example, a twelve-year-old boy was having both academic and behavioral problems and was suspended from school several times. The youngster was referred for a psychological evaluation, and both parents readily participated in the testing and in the counseling, although they had been divorced for several years.

• Visitation is usually a happier occasion if it operates like clock-work—if it is reliable and predictable, especially during the first year or so after the divorce. That is, the best bet is to set up a schedule months ahead of time and then stick to it. The visitation should be planned for specific days and specific times. The visitation should start on time and end on time. This kind of rigid visitation schedule is helpful during the first year of the divorce because it means there is one less issue to discuss and argue about. After everyone has become more comfortable with their new roles, it is possible to be more flexible with the visitation schedule.

• It seems odd that a minor illness, such as a runny nose or a low fever, should prevent visitation from occurring. It seems to me that the noncustodial parent should be encouraged to take care of the child both in sickness and in health.

• It should be obvious that parents, grandparents, and other interested parties should not try to influence and mentally intimidate the children. Even though children are a captive audience, parents should forego the temptation to engage in any form of indoctrination or brainwashing. Fortunately, some children are able to protect themselves from indoctrination. With appropriate discussion and support, such children are able to ignore these malicious activities.

• If a mother thinks that the father may have abused the child, what should she do? Before running off to the Rape Crisis Center, consider what you would have done if you were still married. You probably would

16

have sat down and directly asked the other parent what had happened. One time a little girl told her mother, the custodial parent, that her daddy had hurt her peepee during the weekend visitation. The mother looked and, sure enough, the girl's genital area was red. The mother called protective services and an investigation was undertaken. The child was interviewed by a social worker and a police officer. Eventually the father was contacted and interviewed. He said that over the weekend he had noticed that his daughter had a diaper rash. He consulted the pediatrician, who recommended an ointment. He thought that the ointment may have hurt the child a little when he put it on her. The pediatrician confirmed this account. It would have saved everybody a lot of trouble if the worried mother had simply checked with the father in the first place and asked him what happened over the weekend.

• Parents should try to communicate and agree as much as possible—such as whether the child is going to take ballet or tap-dancing this year; whether the child's attention-deficit problem is severe enough to try him on medication; whether the youngster is allowed to see PG-13 movies. The actual nature of the communication depends on the amount of trust and respect between the parents. If there is still a good deal of anger or friction, it will work better to use regular written communication, perhaps every couple of weeks. But send the notes through the mail, not hand-delivered by the child.

• If the parents cannot agree on some items, they should consider dividing up the decisions and allowing each parent to take responsibility for specific issues. For example, the mother might be totally in charge of the child's birthday party this year; the father will be totally in charge of the science fair project. Or it could be vice versa. The point is that it does not matter so much which parent is going to do which aspect of parenting, but to agree on a division of labor and then stick to it.

• Another way to avoid conflict is for each parent to make plans and arrangements in a way that does not involve the other parent. A noncustodial parent might work with the child in developing a particular interest or hobby (dinosaurs, cooking, rock collecting, whatever) in a way does not need to involve the custodial parent.

• A way to act independently and avoid conflict is for the noncustodial parent to pay for some expenses directly, without going through the custodial parent. If the child is in a private school, for instance, the noncustodial parent can pay her part of the tuition directly to the school rather than to the custodial parent.

• Some of these suggestions seem contradictory. That's right! Sometimes it is better to discuss, negotiate, and agree. Other times it is better for divorced parents to divide the tasks of child rearing and work independently. Parents need to figure out which approach to use in different circumstances. In all cases, however, the underlying motivation is for both parents to be involved and to protect the child from conflict.

• At times divorced parents are not able to work out these issues on their own. They may need professional assistance—such as educational programs for divorced parents; counseling by a mental health professional; or divorce mediation. These topics are discussed in chapter thirteen ("Mental Health Professionals") and in chapter fourteen ("Divorce Mediation").

• Finally, parents might be able to reduce arguing by being flexible and creative in designing the basic custody arrangement. They might consider shared custody, in which the children live in one house during the week and in the other house on weekends. If there are several children, they might consider allowing some of the children to live primarily with one parent and some of the children to live primarily with the other parent. The reason that these unusual arrangements reduce the strife is because they tend to empower both parents more equally. That is, they help both parents feel like full-time, contributing parents, and the result is that there is less arguing about each other's territory. "Uncommon Custody Arrangements" are discussed in chapter four.

The message of this chapter is simple enough. Children of divorce can usually handle the reality that Mom and Dad are not going to be living together any more. They can usually handle the confusion and inconvenience of having a somewhat complicated schedule during the course of the week or the month. They can usually handle the knowledge that their parents disagree at times. What they cannot handle easily are the incessant arguing and the intense fighting. There are many ways for thoughtful parents to reduce the amount of conflict that their children experience.

Chapter Three
Common Custody Arrangements

Giacomo Puccini's famous opera, Madama Butterfly, *is extremely senti-mental and extremely sad. The story line of the opera was actually a custody dispute in the nineteenth century, when it was assumed that the father had an absolute right to have custody of the child.*

The opera was set in Nagasaki, Japan, in the mid-nineteenth century. An officer in the United States Navy, Lieutenant Benjamin Franklin Pin-kerton, arrived at the port city of Nagasaki and married a Japanese woman, Madama Butterfly. They conceived a son, whose name was Trou-ble. Lieutenant Pinkerton promptly sailed back to the United States and left his wife to be the primary—in fact, the exclusive—caretaker of their son. Butterfly raised the child in an adoring manner and waited patiently for the father's return to the family.

After three years Pinkerton did return. But in the meantime he had married an American woman, named Kate, and he had the nerve to bring her with him when he returned to Japan! It soon becomes clear that Lieutenant Pinkerton and his new wife had come to Nagasaki simply to pick up the child and take him away. Butterfly was, of course, devastated. In one short scene, she realized that she no longer had a husband, that his new wife was standing in her living room, and that she was about to lose her cherished son.

Butterfly told Pinkerton and Kate to leave her alone with Trouble for a few minutes, and then they could come and take the child. In the last moments of the opera, Butterfly sat Trouble down, blindfolded him, and put a little American flag in his hands. Then she killed herself. At that moment, Lieutenant Pinkerton returned to see Butterfly's death and to take the child whom he had demanded.

A Short History of Child Custody

In the nineteenth century divorce was infrequent and when it did occur, it was usually assumed that the father would have custody of the children. The husband had control over the marital property and that concept included the children. In *Madama Butterfly*, it was simply taken for granted that the father had the right to possess the little boy, even though he had not laid eyes on Trouble for three years.

In the twentieth century, divorce became more common and courts held that children should generally be raised by their mothers. The notion seemed to be that husbands/fathers would be more likely to be working and were not available to raise the children; that wives/mothers were more likely to be homemakers and were also more nurturing, which young children need. That was called the "tender years doctrine," that mothers were considered better qualified to raise children than fathers were.

In the latter part of the twentieth century occurred women's liberation (so they were more likely to have careers and be working full-time) and also men's liberation (so they were more likely to insist on being full-fledged nurturing parents). The end result was that most courts came to think that the mother and father should have an equal opportunity to be the custodial parent. However, many people still think that very young children, such as infants, are more appropriately raised by their mothers.

In the twenty-first century, who knows what will become of the nuclear family unit and what will be considered normal parenting arrangements? The prevalence of divorce will probably continue to increase. Hopefully, parents and society in general will find ways to nurture the many children of divorced parents.

The Traditional Custodial Parent

The most common arrangement in our society is for one parent to become the permanent custodial parent and for the other to be the noncustodial parent. The children, of course, live primarily with the custodial parent, but have regular visitation with the noncustodial parent. The basic reasoning for this arrangement is that it is important for children to feel that they have a definite, permanent home; to have consistent parenting by the same individual; and to develop roots by living in the same community among the same close friends and relatives. It is also important for the

There are resources for parents who want further information about custodial arrangements and how they come about. A book that is almost a classic is *Mom's House, Dad's House,* by Isolina Ricci (New York: MacMillan, 1980). A more controversial book is *Joint Custody and Shared Parenting,* edited by Jay Folberg (Washington, D.C.: Bureau of National Affairs, 1984). Other possibilities are *Divorcing,* by Melvin Belli and Mel Krantzler (New York: St. Martin's Press, 1988) and *Parent vs. Parent: How You and Your Child Can Survive the Custody Battle,* by Stephen Herman (New York: Pantheon Books, 1990).

children to have a fulfilling, satisfying relationship with the noncustodial parent, so visitation should be endorsed, encouraged, and facilitated by the custodial parent.

In this common, standard custody arrangement, the custodial parent has the responsibility and the authority to make the major decisions regarding the child. That would include decisions such as school placement, medical care, and whether the child should be in counseling for an emotional problem. In practice, the custodial parent usually controls many details of the child's life, such as who his friends are, what his hobbies might be, and how much homework he does every night.

In many divorced families, the custodial and the noncustodial parents raise the children in a reasonably harmonious manner and the children thrive. The children find ways to relate to both parents, to identify with both parents, and to learn from both parents. This arrangement works when the parents put effort into communicating with each other regarding the children, even though they may be bitter toward each other regarding other issues. It works when the divorced mother and father retain a certain amount of respect for each other as parents, even though they detest each other as spouses. Finally, it works when there is some balance between the rights/prerogatives/responsibilities of the custodial and noncustodial parents. That topic is discussed in detail in chapter ten, "Noncustodial Parents."

Joint Custody

Some judges and attorneys and therapists have considered joint custody to be a panacea, that joint custody would be a way for divorced parents to raise the children in a cooperative manner and for both parents to think of themselves as fully involved in important decisions. In joint custody both parents have the authority to make major decisions, such as enrolling the child in a particular school and giving permission for major surgery. The underlying assumption in joint custody is that major decisions will be discussed by the parents and that they will try to reach a consensus on what to do.

Even in situations where the parents have agreed to joint custody, the actual living arrangement for the children is the same as was described above under the "traditional" plan. That is, the children usually live in one parent's household most of the time and have regular visitations to the other household. The fact that two parents have joint custody does not make the task of raising the children any easier. They must still put effort into communicating and have some degree of respect for each other as parents. Joint custody is a good way for some divorcing parents to raise the children together. However, it is unlikely that joint custody is the solution to any divorce that is extremely hostile and adversarial.

Practically any arrangement works if the divorcing parents have based it on mutual respect for each other and are willing to work out the details. There is, however, an important exception to the general principle that practically anything will work if both parents agree. That is, children can figure it out when the parents are cooperating in an effort to achieve what is convenient for themselves rather than what is good for the children. Sometimes divorced parents agree to joint custody and then divide the children's time between the two households in a way that simply suits the convenience of the parents. The parents may be doing this because neither of them really wants to take on full responsibility for the children.

Chapter Four
Uncommon Custody Arrangements

Mr. Stevens and Ms. Stevens had a somewhat unusual experience in the evolution of their custody arrangement. Like many divorcing parents, they both desired permanent custody of all the children. They had three sons: Tom, twelve; Dick, eight; and Harry, six. Although they were not viciously angry at each other, they did fight it out in court and the judge awarded custody to the mother. The judge probably considered it a close call. The mother had been a homemaker and the primary caretaker during the marriage. However, she was chronically depressed and had even been hospitalized on one occasion when she was considered suicidal. The father was eager to raise the boys, but his time was limited because he was a successful and extremely busy architect.

What was unusual about the situation was that the oldest boy, Tom, was difficult to parent because he was impulsive, hyperactive, and had a severe learning disability. He attended a specialized school program for children with learning disabilities and emotional problems. When he was home, he required a great deal of adult attention and a careful blend of both structure and nurturance. The mother had her hands full trying to raise these three boys. As a single parent, it was extremely hard for her to meet the needs of the two "normal" children as well as her handicapped son. The mother's household was chaotic because there was constant friction between Tom and his mother (who found it hard to set consistent limits with him) and between Tom and his brothers (who resented how much of the mother's time he consumed). Ms. Stevens became frustrated and more depressed; Tom became dangerously impulsive; and the younger boys, Dick and Harry, felt angry and neglected.

Mr. Stevens, meanwhile, was thinking about going back to court and threatened to subpoena Ms. Stevens's psychiatrist in order to prove that the mother was too disturbed to be considered a competent custodial parent. A mediator worked with the parents to see if they could find a reasonable solution that did not involve further litigation. The mediator helped the parents arrive at an arrangement that seemed workable: that the mother would continue to be the custodial parent for Dick and Harry and the father would become the custodial parent for Tom.

This new arrangement worked out better for everybody. The father found a specialized after-school program for Tom, so he was adequately supervised. The father felt that he truly had a role in raising his sons. The mother easily managed Dick and Harry and started to feel like a competent parent again. Visitation was scheduled in a way that the three siblings were frequently able to be together.

Separating the siblings into different custodial households is an uncommon outcome of custody disputes. That approach and other unusual custody arrangements will be discussed in this chapter. The message of this chapter is that there are many different circumstances in divorced families. The parents themselves may have widely different skills, attitudes, and interests when it comes to rearing children. There are many details that should be considered in determining what would be the best living arrangements for the children in a divorced family. The parameters that might be important include the attitudes of the parents; the physical and mental health of the parents; the work schedules of the parents; the role of stepparents and extended family members; the neighborhoods where they live; the attachments that the children have to the two parents; and the preferences that the children may express. There are so many circumstances that might be important, that it seems obvious that there might be many different kinds of custody arrangements.

Anything Goes . . . Almost

Practically any arrangement works if the divorcing parents have taken three important principles into consideration. First, the plan should be derived primarily from the needs of the children rather than from the schedule that is most convenient for the parents. Second, the parents should have some sense of mutual respect for each other, rather than feeling that one parent is trying to take advantage of the other. Finally, it is important to communicate to work out the details.

24

Divorcing parents have devised many custody and visitation plans that may seem unusual. For example:

• Some parents have retained the family home, and each parent also rented a small apartment for his or her own use. In other words, the children continued to live all the time in exactly the same place. During most of the week, the custodial parent lived with the children in the family home and the noncustodial parent lived in his apartment. During visitation time, the custodial parent stayed in her apartment and the noncustodial parent lived with the children in the family home.

• Rather than have weekend visitation, some parents have agreed that the children would live with the custodial parent for three weeks straight and then with the noncustodial parent for one full week. That would work if the parents live near each other and it is convenient to go to school and to other regular activities from both households.

• In another family, the children lived in each household half the time. That is, they lived six months with one parent and then six months with the other parent. Of course, during both halves of the year, the children had visitation with the parent they were not living with.

• Unusual visitation schedules also occur when the parents live in distant cities. The parents might agree that the children would spend the entire school year with one parent and the winter vacation and summer vacation with the other parent.

These unusual custody and visitation arrangements work because parents go into them with both eyes open and with some willingness to cooperate and negotiate with the former spouse. In my experience, courts approve almost any arrangement that has been worked out between the parents, unless it is obviously harmful to the children.

This chapter examines in detail two uncommon custody arrangements, referred to here as split custody and shared custody. Split custody is the arrangement in which siblings are separated, in that some of them primarily live with the mother and some primarily live with the father. In shared custody, both parents have legal custody of the child. However, one parent may be completely responsible for what happens during the week and the other parent is completely responsible for what happens on weekends. These custody arrangements are uncommon for a reason: most divorcing couples do fine with the traditional models discussed in chapter three. It is important, however, for some divorced parents to consider less common custody arrangements, such as split custody and shared custody.

Asking the Right Question

In the vignette at the beginning of this chapter, the Stevenses found themselves with a tough situation. Initially they were asking themselves and also asking the court a particular question: "Is Mr. Stevens or Ms. Stevens better equipped to be the custodial parent of the three boys, Tom, Dick, and Harry?" As time went on, they later were asking a different question: "How can two concerned parents, who are divorced, find a way to raise three boys, who demand an unusual degree of parental nurturing and supervision?" In the illustration, the Stevenses eventually agreed to separate the boys and divide the custody, so that the father became the primary parent for Tom and the mother continued to be the primary parent for Dick and Harry.

It is unusual for parents to take that step. It is also unusual for judges to separate children in making a decision in a custody case. In some states, case law has established a presumption that siblings should stay together, so a judge would have to have a very good reason to override that legal precedent. I think that in some families—although this does not occur very often—it is in the best interests of both the children and the parents for the siblings to be separated and the custody to be divided between the two parents.

Before we try to create an exception to the rule, we should try to understand why it is advantageous in most families to keep the children together. There have been several reasons for having such a strong presumption that siblings should be kept together. First of all, divorce is extremely stressful for the children. During this time in which children feel threatened, insecure, and wounded, they need all the support and consistency they can find. Many children feel more comforted and more comfortable when all the brothers and sisters are living together. They have the sense that at least that part of the family is still in one piece. I agree that is an important consideration and is a logical reason for keeping the children together.

The second reason for assuming that siblings should stay together is also logical. That is, some siblings naturally form pairs or groups because of their gender and birth order. Two boys who are twelve and fourteen years old are likely to have a great many interests in common and are likely to be extremely important to each other, even if they are fussing and feuding much of the time. It makes sense in such a family to have a presumption that the siblings would be together. In another family, the children might form quite distinct groups: a divorcing couple could have two sons who are fourteen and fifteen and two daughters who are seven and eight. In that family, the parents might agree for the father to be the custodial parent for the boys and the mother to be the custodial parent for the girls.

Fallacious Reasoning

I can understand and support the two explanations that I have just mentioned for keeping the siblings together. What concerns me is that courts seem to go beyond those reasons and to assume that siblings should *always* be kept together. In being so arbitrary and so rigid, they seem to be basing their conclusions not only on the two legitimate reasons, but on two additional fallacious reasons.

The first fallacious reason for keeping the siblings together is a result of the usual practice of creating a contest in order to figure out which parent would make the better custodial parent. When one is working within the context of a contest, the result is that the winner takes everything. Think about it: if the father, for instance, is found to be a "better person" and therefore the preferred parent for child A, then he obviously is going to be the preferred parent for children B, C, and D as well. Many judges would be likely to view these situations simplistically and decide that one parent has won the case and therefore that parent should have custody of all the children. Although this reason seems superficially logical, it really does not make sense. The issues in most divorced families are quite complex, and it may well be that one parent will be better at raising the first child and the other parent better at raising the second child.

The second fallacious reason for keeping the siblings together is the mistaken belief that child-care experts have said that it should be done this way. I think that some judges and therapists remember learning in school that the siblings should always be kept together in order to provide mutual support. However, they have mixed up what should be done in custody situations with what should be done in other situations when children have come to the attention of the court and require a placement

27

decision. I am referring to the unfortunate situations in which children have been orphaned or neglected or abused—for whatever reasons, the children are having to be placed in foster care.

Many years ago, child-care agencies dealt with these children like so many numbers and randomly divided them up among available foster homes. It could have happened that children from one family would be removed from both of their parents, because of abuse or neglect, and then removed from each other by placement in different foster homes. Those children would have been totally devastated, having been suddenly removed from their home, their parents, and their siblings. That kind of outcome—tragedy heaped on tragedy—does not happen so much any more because now social service agencies make efforts to keep the siblings together. Some of them have created rules or guidelines that remind them to keep the siblings together whenever possible.

During the last ten or twenty years, the rule—*"always* keep the siblings together"—has spread from cases that involved foster home placement to cases that involve custody disputes. I do not think that these situations are comparable. Children of divorce have not suddenly lost the love and the availability of both parents. They usually still have two devoted parents, who happen to live in different homes. Even if the children live in two households, they are still going to see both parents and all their brothers and sisters on a regular schedule. Although there are reasons to keep the children of divorce together in the same custodial household, it should not be thought an absolute rule that never provides room for exceptions.

Separating the Siblings

Sometimes the arrangement in which the siblings are separated is called split custody. It should be understood that if children are divided between the two parents, the children continue to be together in the same household more than half the time. The visitation schedule between the two homes can be arranged so that the children are together five days out of seven. The typical schedule for a school-aged child is to visit the noncustodial parent every other weekend, from Friday evening to Sunday evening, and also one weekday evening every week. The example that follows of John and Mary shows how it would turn out if a divorced couple decided to divide the custody of their children. For the sake of simplicity, we will say that the father has custody of John and the mother has custody of Mary.

The location of the two children over a two-week period of time is summarized in the box on the next page. In the two-week cycle in the example, Mary had her weekend visit with the father on the first weekend. John had his weekend visit with the mother on the second weekend. In addition to the every other weekend visitation, they have agreed that John visits the mother's home every Wednesday evening and that Mary visits the father's home every Tuesday evening. By arranging the schedule in a reciprocal manner, the children are actually living together in the same household every single weekend and two evenings during the week. The only waking times that they would routinely be away from each other are Monday evenings and Thursday evenings. In fact, that is not a bad outcome either, because it would seem to make sense to have an arrangement that allows each child to have some individual time with a parent.

Shared Custody

Another uncommon custody arrangement is what I call shared custody. In some ways it is similar to joint custody, but it has features that may be important in situations where traditional joint custody does not work. In shared custody, one parent is completely in charge of school activities and the child lives with that parent on weekdays. The second parent is completely in charge of church and other events, such as the child's participation in Little League, that happen on the weekends. The parents are not expected to seek the other person's opinion or agreement, since each parent has the authority to make the decisions regarding his or her area or responsibility.

Shared custody, as described here, is not appropriate for most divorcing parents. If the two parents communicate well with each other and respect each other's opinions and feelings, they would do better with traditional joint custody. If one parent is clearly a better choice because that parent is much more competent or has a much better relationship with the child, it would probably be better to have the common arrangement of a custodial and a noncustodial parent.

Shared custody should be considered if both parents have significant strengths and weaknesses and if neither parent appears ready and able to take full responsibility for the child. Also, it should be considered if both

	Dad's House	Mom's House
Monday	John	Mary
Tuesday	John, Mary	
Wednesday		John, Mary
Thursday	John	Mary
Friday	John, Mary	
Saturday	John, Mary	
Sunday	John, Mary	
Monday	John	Mary
Tuesday	John, Mary	
Wednesday		John, Mary
Thursday	John	Mary
Friday		John, Mary
Saturday		John, Mary
Sunday		John, Mary

This table shows that John and Mary would be together most of the time, even though they primarily live in different households.

parents need to take a major share of child-rearing responsibility, but they are not willing to communicate and confer with each other. For example, shared parenting should be considered if one parent happens to be very good at monitoring the child's schoolwork in an orderly and helpful manner and if the other parent happens to be very good at creating and supervising recreational activities. It should be considered if the parents both work and have complementary schedules, such that one parent always works during the week and the other one always works on weekends.

Disclaimer

Divorcing parents can choose among a wide range of custody arrangements for their children. Some of the custody plans discussed in chapter three and in this chapter are quite different from each other. The point is that parents and attorneys and judges should think about these issues in ways that are creative and that are adapted to each family's individual situation.

My disclaimer is that I am not trying to suggest that any custody or visitation system at all is going to work smoothly. Parents have come up with ideas that are very impracticable. Courts have been known to impose unusual custody plans and certain restrictions on visitation that are doomed to failure because they are extremely arbitrary; because they give an unusual advantage to one of the parents; or because they ignore the developmental needs of the children. For instance, one judge said that the noncustodial parent could have visitation with his children absolutely any weekend he wanted, as long as he gave sixty days notice to the custodial parent. The problem was that the noncustodial parent was in the military and it was very hard for him to plan that far ahead; on some occasions he planned the visit three months ahead, but he was not granted leave when the actual weekend arrived.

Chapter three and chapter four have described four types of custody arrangements: the traditional plan with the custodial parent and the non-custodial parent; joint custody, in which both parents have legal authority to make decisions; split custody, in which siblings live in different primary households; and shared custody, in which each parent has primary responsibility for different parts of the child's life. Having considered the basic structure, we now move on to the day-to-day and week-to-week details of parenting the children of divorce.

Chapter Five

Balancing the Needs of Parents and Children

Two parents, who were both successful professionals, consulted a therapist who was experienced in custody and visitation evaluations. The parents were in the process of divorcing and said they both wanted to do what was best for their two daughters, Merrie and Melodie. Merrie was sixteen and Melodie was twelve. They both expressed the lofty view that they did not want to take the other parent to court and have a big custody battle, but they wanted to work out what was best for the girls in a rational and cooperative manner. They both were concerned that the girls were already distraught over the divorce and were manifesting symptoms. That is, Merrie was acting out sexually and Melodie was depressed and alluding to suicidal ideation.

The parents explained the plan that they had already worked out between themselves. Both of them had important careers and both wanted to continue to work full-time. They had agreed on a schedule in which both daughters would alternate between the mother's household and the father's household on a weekly basis. They had agreed on joint custody, so that each parent would be fully responsible for the girls when they were with that parent.

The therapist interviewed Merrie and Melodie separately and also together. They both were angry and miserable. They strongly resented the arrangement in which they had to live in two different households. The girls did not seem distressed about the divorce itself. They had strong attachments to both parents and were perfectly willing to live with either their mother or father. What they resented was having to live half the time in each household. They had figured out that the parents were putting their own desires above the needs of the girls.

The therapist met again with the parents and determined the basic issue in the case, that neither parent was willing to take charge of the situation and to provide a full-time home for their daughters. Both parents really wanted the other parent to take full custody of Merrie and Melodie. The therapist explained his assessment of the girls, that their symptoms were related to feeling rejected and being repeatedly displaced on a week-to-week basis. The therapist was able to propose some other options for the parents to consider. One possibility was the traditional arrangement of one parent working only part-time and being able to raise the children. The parent who continued to work full-time would, of course, provide child support. A second possibility was for the girls to alternate on a much longer cycle, such as every six months or once a year. A third possibility was for each parent to be the primary parent for one child. That is, Merrie could live with the father and visit the mother; Melodie could live with the mother and visit the father.

This chapter is about parents who avoid their basic responsibilities to the children. They are putting their own needs above the needs of the children. The usual scenario in custody and visitation disputes is that one or both parents are trying to take something away from the other parent. That is, Parent A is trying to take custody away from Parent B or trying to limit Parent B's visitation. In the family of Merrie and Melodie, however, both parents were trying to push more visitation and more responsibility off onto the other parent. Merrie and Melodie were the victims of a reverse custody dispute.

Sometimes the phenomenon of the reverse custody dispute is apparent to all. It is like O. Henry's famous story: in "The Ransom of Red Chief," kidnappers had taken a very demanding and very obnoxious little boy, who was the son of a wealthy banker. The child was so disagreeable that the kidnappers eventually were willing to pay the father to take the child back.

In the case of Merrie and Melodie, the process was more subtle. In fact, what was interesting was the disguise that the mother and father had developed. The parents had colluded in a way to look like they were only concerned about the girls' welfare, that is, for the girls to have a continuing relationship with both mother and father. In fact, what the parents really had in mind was to avoid providing what the girls really needed, a consistent household.

Divorced parents may find many ways to put their own interests and needs above those of the children. As far as they are concerned, divorce means to find a way to achieve "the best interests of the parents." The reverse custody dispute is one way, in which the parents maneuver in a way to take less responsibility for the children. This chapter will also describe blatant and subtle ways in which parents neglect their children's needs.

Blatant Neglect by Divorced Parents

It is fortunately uncommon that parents actively shun responsibility for their children. It may happen, however, when a parent is irresponsible and puts personal desires and conveniences above the needs of the child. A parent who has a serious alcohol or drug problem may be temporarily oblivious to the physical safety and other needs of the child. On the other hand, a single parent may not be irresponsible, but just overwhelmed. For instance, a parent might find an unusually difficult child to be emotionally draining and may eventually tune out the child's requests for nurturance, for attention, and simply for dinner.

A divorced individual may find that the demands of an active social life compromises his or her responsibilities as a parent. This criticism is made more often about mothers. A divorced mother may very much want to develop a relationship with a new boyfriend. She may invite the boyfriend to move in with her. She may end up with a long series of boyfriends who have moved in. The children in her household would certainly be bumped to the bottom of her list of priorities.

Another rather blatant form of neglect is to include the children in the parent's partying. This seems to happen more with single parents, perhaps because two parents who are together are more likely to police each other. In any case, what happens is that friends congregate at the parent's home and the partying gets under way. Under the best of these circumstances, the children are passive observers of the grown-ups' activities. When the situation deteriorates further, the adults give drugs to the children and may sexually abuse them.

The Disappearing Parent

A noncustodial parent may neglect his or her children by disappearing—a rather clear message that the parent considers his or her needs

Although it is generally agreed that in a custody dispute everybody should be working toward the best interests of the child, life is not always so simple. Frequently courts must consider the legal rights of the biological parents and the rights of the psychological parents (who might be somebody else), as well as the child's best interests. A dramatic example of that kind of problem was the dispute between Daniel and Cara Schmidt, who lived in Iowa, and Jan and Roberta DeBoer, who lived in Michigan. Their little girl was the biological child of the Schmidts, but she had lived since birth with the DeBoers. The DeBoers were undoubtedly the girl's psychological parents. The courts in both states thought that the rights of the biological parents should be taken into consideration, even if those rights might conflict with the best interests of the child. The concept of the psychological parent was explained in an important book, *Beyond the Best Interests of the Child* (New York: Free Press, 1973), that was written by Joseph Goldstein, Anna Freud, and Albert Solnit.

more important than what might be good for the child. When I do psychiatric custody evaluations, I sometimes ask both parents what they will do if the court decides the case in favor of the other parent. One time a mother told me that if she lost the custody battle she would move to Oregon and never see her children again. I thought she might have misunderstood the question, so I asked her again. She assured me that she was convinced that if she could not have total control of her children, she had no interest in having any relationship with them at all. For anybody who reads this book and happens to see a mental health professional for a psychiatric custody evaluation, that was the *wrong answer.* I thought that the mother's response graphically displayed how her own emotional needs were more important than her relationship with the children.

Sadly, many noncustodial parents do drop out of sight. They move away, perhaps remarry, and move on with their lives in a way that does not include their children. What seems worse is the noncustodial parent who intermittently disappears, but surfaces often enough to tease the child in a way that is downright mean. These parents have a way of telephoning a few weeks before Christmas or before the child's birthday and they promise that some special present is going to arrive for the child. The child, of course, gets his hopes up and then is disappointed over and over.

Subtle Neglect by Divorced Parents

Most of the time, divorced parents are not so obvious in the ways they neglect their children's needs. In fact, sometimes this form of "neglect" actually takes on the appearance of almost limitless affection and concern for the child.

For example, what about the noncustodial mother who seems extremely concerned about how her son Randolph is doing in the second grade? Since the mother does not have custody, she knows that Randolph is missing her dearly and she feels the need to comfort him frequently. In order to check on his schoolwork and to make sure that he isn't missing her too much, the mother starts to phone Randolph every evening around dinner time. By every evening, I mean *every* evening. Since she wants to make sure that he gets off to a good day in school, she starts calling Randolph in the mornings when he is having breakfast. Since she wants him to do his best in school, the mother starts checking with the teacher every week or so. Under the guise of being a nurturing, concerned mother, she may well be hurting Randolph more than helping him. In particular it is likely that she is missing Randolph more than Randolph is missing her. The real purpose of the phone calls is for the mother's reassurance rather than for the child's. What Randolph needs to hear from his mother is that he is a good boy and that he can get along without her for several days or even a week at a time. The way to get that idea across to Randolph is to stop calling him every day.

Or what about the noncustodial father who decides that it is his mission in life to turn his twelve-year-old son, Macon, into a premier student athlete? The father starts to attend every basketball practice and every game. He sits near the bench so that he can give reminders to Macon when he is not actually playing. The father enrolls the boy in the Saturday Scholar program at the local university, so that he can get a head start in computer programming. And for the rest of the weekend, they practice together to be ready for the father-son basketball tournament. Is this merely a dedicated father? Or is this a man who is taking advantage of his son and using the boy to give the father some sense of fulfillment?

Balancing the Needs of Parents and Children

It is easy to criticize parents who are divorced and are trying to balance their own needs as single and perhaps insecure parents with the needs of their children. The basic message here is *not* that divorced parents should be totally selfless in raising their children. The message is *not* that divorced parents should be perfect in resolving the complex issues that come up almost every day. The message is something like this: that raising children is very hard work; that it is even harder when the parents are divorced; that parents do have to expect to make some sacrifices; that divorced parents should strive to find a balance between their own needs as adults and their children's needs; and, especially, that parents should not fool themselves into thinking that their decisions and their behaviors are in the children's interests, when actually they are serving the emotional needs of the parents.

Here are some ways to balance the needs of parents and children. The following suggestions and examples involve some degree of conflict between the interests of the parent and the needs of the child. There is no simple answer to some of these scenarios. The purpose of these examples is not to give cookbook advice for how to deal with complex situations, but to illustrate several ways by which a person might balance these conflicting interests.

- Divorced parents may find it more convenient to deal with their children as a group, all at the same time. Children benefit, however, from sharing some individual time with each parent. One way to do that is to take one child out to do some shopping, while the other child plays at a friend's house. Visitation might be arranged so that, on some occasions, the noncustodial parent only has one child at a time. This requires a greater time commitment by both parents, but it is better for the children.

- Being a single parent can be lonely. It is a common problem for single parents to use their children as buddies, confidants, and soul mates. In one family, a divorced mother was concerned about her son and only child, who was a high-school senior. Although a bright student who had previously done well in school, the youngster was foundering and it looked like he would not be able to go away to college and might not even graduate on time. The mother and boy spent much of their free time together. Their Saturday evening routine was dinner and the theater. A counselor explained firmly that the mother and son needed to separate from each other in the psychological sense. As a starter, they needed to have separate social lives. The mother and boy agreed that they depended too much on each other. After achieving some emotional distance from his mother, the boy did well in school and went away to college.

• When they plan for holidays, divorced parents should think of the needs of the children. That does not refer to purchasing a pile of presents and having a bang-up holiday dinner. When the kids arrive for a Christmas holiday, for example, let them relax and unwind and simply hang out for a while, rather than hustling them off immediately to see the relatives. Holiday celebrations require a lot of preparation and parents sometimes expect children to demonstrate their appreciation in an explicit manner, such as saying, "Thank you very much" after each present is opened. It is better for a parent to feel satisfied and appreciated by simply enjoying a good time together with his children, rather than waiting for those "thank yous."

• In Los Angeles, two divorced parents had an adult son who had cystic fibrosis. Cystic fibrosis is a chronic illness that gradually destroyed the child's lungs. In fact, he was about to die. In an unusual operation, surgeons transplanted parts of the lungs of both parents into their son's chest in order to save his life. According to a newspaper report, the parents, who had divorced seventeen years previously, held hands on the way to the surgery. Most divorced parents do not have such dramatic roles to play, but they still struggle with how to balance their personal needs with their child's welfare.

The most important consideration in providing for the emotional needs of children of divorce is to protect the child from parental battles. That is, parents may need to be less demanding and less self-centered in order to avoid fighting over the children, through the children, and in front of the children. The second consideration is to find a balance between the needs of the children and the needs of the parents. Happily, many times children and their parents need exactly the same thing, but often it is necessary to work out compromises and set priorities. The third consideration in addressing the emotional needs of these children can be quite challenging—helping the child have loving and satisfying relationships with both parents. That is the subject of the next chapter, "Trying to Love Both Parents."

Chapter Six
Trying to Love Both Parents

Annie and Danny were young teenagers who lived with their father. Their parents had divorced when they were in elementary school. The father had obtained permanent custody of both children at the time, primarily because the mother was having some medical problems that prevented her from putting very much energy into the rearing of the two active, boisterous, and somewhat demanding children.

When her health improved, the mother went back to court and requested that both children be transferred to her custody. She had a vigorous attorney who argued in a vigorous manner that there had been a change of circumstances, that is, that the mother's health had improved and she was now available to be a fully competent full-time parent. The attorney also argued vigorously that since the mother was not employed, she was even more available than the father to nurture and supervise Annie and Danny. Finally, the attorney learned that Danny had been in counseling and he subpoenaed the therapist's notes. The attorney discovered that the counseling had started because there had been some conflict between Danny and his father, so that provided even more ammunition for the mother's case.

The legal process went on for about six months, from the time that the mother originally filed her custody suit to the time the court made its decision to leave Annie and Danny in the custody of their father. The court felt that it was better to leave well enough alone because the children seemed to be thriving in the father's household; because they were behaving about as well as young adolescents usually behave; and because both children expressed a preference to leave the custody arrangement the way it had been.

During the six months of legal wrangling, the family's activities remained the same. That is, the children were living with the father and had regular visitation with the mother, every other weekend from Friday

evening to Sunday evening. Annie and Danny enjoyed riding and groom-
ing the horse that the mother kept. The children and the mother had
created a tradition of seeing every new horror movie at the local multiplex
theater, which they all enjoyed. During that time, however, Danny became
less enthusiastic about planning activities for the visitation. He started
to find reasons to postpone the visitations or to return home early. He
stopped initiating phone calls to his mother, and he seemed to lack inter-
est in pleasing her or spending time with her. Several months after the
court case ended, Danny refused to visit his mother at all.

With that turn of events, Danny was taken again to see his therapist.
The therapist was puzzled, because there was no obvious reason for the
boy's intense alienation from his mother. Had the mother intimidated or
pressured him during the court case? Danny said no. Had either parent
been saying bad things about the other parent? The youngster did not
describe any form of bad-mouthing or indoctrination, but simply said
that he was aware of the anger and tension between the parents. Had
the father been suggesting, even in a subtle manner, that Danny did not
need to visit the mother so often? No, said Danny. In fact, the father had
persistently encouraged both children to continue the visitation at the
scheduled times every other weekend. As the therapist got a little more
desperate to find an explanation for Danny's refusal of visitation, he
started to wonder if the boy had been traumatized in some way, but had
kept it secret. He eventually came right out and asked if Danny had been
physically abused or sexually molested at the mother's house, which the
boy denied. The therapist even investigated if the child could have been
hypnotized by the father, which seemed unlikely.

Danny's refusal to visit his mother was stated adamantly, but was
supported by vague reasons. The child simply said that he had other
more important things to do, that he did not particularly enjoy being with
his mother, that he didn't think that she understood him, that she didn't
treat him right, that he didn't see any point to having a relationship with
his mother, and so on. Danny's explanations were vague because he
himself did not really understand what had happened to him. His subjec-
tive experience was simply that he had a perfectly good relationship
with his father and that he did not find it pleasant to spend time with
his mother.

The story about Danny illustrates something that happens often
enough, that a child of divorced parents becomes strongly alienated from

one of the parents, usually the noncustodial parent. For the child, the affection he has for the "alien parent" is about the same as he feels for some distant relative or for some neighbor down the street. He does not experience a sense of attachment, and he finds that parent's expressions of affection to be intrusive and annoying.

What is this phenomenon and why does it happen? Therapists and attorneys who work with divorced parents and their children have seen many examples of this condition, which often are more heartbreaking than the story about Danny. The usual explanation for parental alienation is that the custodial parent has actively brainwashed the child into disliking the other parent. I am sure that indoctrination does happen in some divorced families and that it leads to parental alienation. However, I think that there is another explanation for this condition, which does not involve indoctrination at all. Basically, it is very hard for a child to love both parents when he knows that the parents are angrily fighting with each other. Both of these methods for arriving at parent alienation will be discussed in this chapter.

The terms "indoctrination" and "parental alienation" are both somewhat pejorative. They both suggest that there has been a malicious person who has actively induced the child to dislike one of the parents. The former term certainly requires that someone actually did the indoctrination. The latter term suggests that somebody actively alienated the child from one of the parents. A more neutral way to think about parental alienation is simply to think of the child as having already made up his mind. The child who has completely made up his mind about his feelings about his parents may have been influenced by an active, malicious process ("parental alienation through indoctrination") or may have been influenced by his exposure to specific adversarial conditions ("parental alienation without indoctrination").

Parental Alienation through Indoctrination

This process is quite easy to understand and is sometimes easy to detect. It may occur when one parent is still very angry at her former spouse and she takes advantage of her role as the custodial parent to induce the child to criticize and dislike the noncustodial parent. Since the custodial parent has almost total control over what the child hears, thinks, and feels, she can use that power to help the child believe that she is a wonderful parent and that the father is a bum. (Please do not assume that mothers do this any more than fathers, just because this section is written with feminine pronouns. This material is easier to follow if the custodial parent is taken to be the mother.)

Most indoctrination is done in a fairly subtle manner. That is, I doubt that the mother simply sits the child down and says, "I want you to hate Daddy because he is wicked." What actually happens is probably more low-key and takes place over a period of time. The mother might make many statements that seem to be supportive and sympathetic to the beleaguered child and that also suggest a special relationship between the child and the mother. For instance:

"I'm sorry that Daddy spanked you at his house yesterday. Let me give you a big hug."

"It's too bad that you have to spend Christmas with Daddy's family. You remember what your grandmother said to you last year."

"I'm going to miss you so much when you're at Daddy's house for the weekend. Be sure to call me Saturday evening to make sure that I'm okay."

"Did Daddy hurt your peepee when he gave you a bath last night? I hope he wasn't mean to you."

Keep up those comments for a few weeks and you will probably have a child who feels that her mother is the only person in the world who really loves her; who is convinced that her father is a mean, violent, dangerous person to be feared and avoided; and who has concluded that the only course of action is to become oppositional and hysterical when her father comes to pick her up for visitation.

The child who has been alienated through indoctrination is often quite willing to share his or her opinions and attitudes with other people. For instance, such a child may be taken to a mental health professional for evaluation because of a strong reluctance to visit the other parent. Sometimes it is quite obvious in the interview that the custodial parent has programmed the child to say specific things to the evaluator. For instance, in the initial meeting, the counselor asked the child what the mother had told him to say. The boy responded, "Mommy told me to tell you about all the times that Daddy spanked me with a belt and shut me in a closet."

On another occasion a mother had attempted to give more subtle instructions to her child, who said, "Mommy said not to make Daddy sound any worse than he really is!" Finally, some programmed children

42

Richard Gardner, M.D., is a child psychiatrist who has helped to define the meaning of parental alienation. He has published several books related to this subject: *Family Evaluation in Child Custody Litigation* (Cresskill, N.J.: Creative Therapeutics, 1982); *Psychotherapy with Children of Divorce* (Northvale, N.J.: Jason Aronson, 1991); and *The Parental Alienation Syndrome* (Cresskill, N.J.: Creative Therapeutics, 1992). Dr. Gardner has divided the cases of parental alienation into three types—mild, moderate, and severe—and that determination helps the therapist know what approach to use in counseling.

Another book on this topic is *Children Held Hostage: Dealing with Programmed and Brainwashed Children* (Chicago: American Bar Association, 1991). It was written by Stanley Clawar and Brynne Rivlin and it presents many examples of how parents indoctrinate their children.

sound like little tape recorders. A counselor asked a boy what he had been doing since his last visit. He responded, ''I went to the beach with my mother and I played with my mother in the sand and then I played with my Aunt Agnes in the water and I had a very good time.'' When asked what happened after that, the boy repeated, ''I went to the beach with my mother and I played with my mother in the sand and then I played with Aunt Agnes in the water and I had a very good time.''

Sometimes children who have been instructed and programmed to recite criticisms of the noncustodial parent behave in a quite surprising manner when they actually do have visitation. There may be some initial resistance, especially when the custodial parent who did the programming is still in sight, but after a few minutes, the child is perfectly happy and cheerful with the noncustodial parent. At the end of the visitation time, the child may once again become petulant and negativistic when the custodial parent comes into view. Basically the child is doing her best to be pleasing to both parents.

The process of parental alienation through indoctrination is easy to understand. The process involves an actual culprit who has programmed the child, and it is usually easy to hear the words of the parent coming from the mouth of the child. In some situations it is possible to interpret the process and to help the child be comfortable with both parents. There is another form of parental alienation that is harder to understand. It may

43

be harder to modify once it is in place in the child's mind. For want of a better term, I refer to it as "parental alienation without indoctrination." Another description could be to say that the adversarial process has caused the child to make up his mind to like one parent and dislike the other one.

Parental Alienation without Indoctrination

The basic issue with this form of parental alienation is that it is hard for a child to maintain affection for two individuals who are persistently and actively fighting with each other. For some children it is not just hard—it is impossible. The result is that the child gravitates to either one parent or the other. The child attaches to and identifies with the chosen parent and assumes an attitude of antipathy and hostility to the rejected parent. When this process occurs, the child usually attaches to and identifies with the parent with whom he lives the most, that is, the custodial parent. That does not seem inevitable, however, since sometimes the child attaches to the missing or the noncustodial parent.

I want to emphasize that I am referring to families where the two divorced parents have almost equal merit. That is, they both have been involved with the child rearing. They both have invested their love and time and energy and money in their relationships with the child. Although not perfect, they both seem like reasonably nice people and competent parents. I am not talking about families where it would be completely understandable for the child to firmly love one parent who is nurturing and sober and to firmly despise another parent who is frequently drunk, angry, and abusive. I am not talking about a family where one parent has been a consistent caretaker and the other parent has been absent for many years. In such families it is easy to see why a child might bond with one parent and reject the other. I am referring to families where both parents have been available and loving with the child, so it is not obvious why the child bonds with one parent and rejects the other. I am referring to cases such as Annie and Danny at the start of this chapter, in which Danny became firmly attached to his father and firmly rejected his mother's affection.

What makes this happen? How does parental alienation occur when both parents have been reasonable people and indoctrination has not occurred? This is a tragic and common situation, and it needs an explanation.

44

This form of alienation occurs in a way that neither the child himself nor the parents notice. They are too close to the situation to see what is happening. But it is important to see that it is almost impossible for a child to love both parents when it is obvious to him that the parents are actively, angrily hating each other. The child's mind is not strong enough or sophisticated enough to be able to love Mom (who hates Dad) and also love Dad (who hates Mom). In fact, it is hard enough for adults to handle relationships such as these. If you are friends with a couple who are involved in an extremely angry divorce, you are likely to continue your friendship with one or the other person, but not with both of them. It would be much harder for a small child to remain on friendly, affectionate terms with two parents who are feuding in a major way. In order for the child to accomplish this feat, he would have to say something like this to himself: "I am going to love the part of Mom that loves me, but ignore the part of her that is fighting with Dad; and I'm going to love that part of Dad that loves me, but ignore the part of him that is fighting with Mom." That's a large order for a small child.

The idea that a child might completely reject a parent through this process, without any active indoctrination or intimidation or coercion, is hard to understand. It is particularly hard for the rejected parent to understand. I will belabor the point with another kind of analogy. A sports fan who lives in Washington, D.C., could easily become an avid and fanatical follower of both the Washington Redskins and the Baltimore Orioles. He could pour an enormous amount of energy and devotion into traveling to games and cheering his teams. He would never experience any form of loyalty conflict because the Redskins and the Orioles never compete against each other. On the other hand, is there any way a football fan could be dedicated to both the Redskins and the Dallas Cowboys? Of course not. In fact, any truly loyal Redskins fan would not be neutral about the Cowboys, but would automatically notice and magnify any blemish or defect or failure that the Cowboys might show. Likewise, a person who is emotionally involved in a highly adversarial situation is likely to gravitate strongly to one side of the conflict and to reject strongly the other side.

This form of parental alienation is not the result of parental indoctrination or coercion, but is a natural outcome of a highly adversarial relationship between the parents. It is usually not caused by either parent alone, but is created by the battle of both parents together. There may be reasons why the child gravitates to a particular parent. One reason is

45

simply that after the divorce the child lived with one parent more than the other and therefore identified with that parent more closely. In other cases the rejected parent actually did something mean at some time in the past. It may have been a rather minor accident, such as giving the child a spanking. But what happens is that the child latches onto that small incident and uses it as his explanation for why he despises and avoids that parent. In other words, the sense of alienation of the rejected parent is quite strong, but the chid has trouble explaining the depth of his feeling. The child's verbal explanations for the alienation usually seem quite trivial and inadequate.

The Continuum of Parental Alienation

In order to explain how parental alienation comes about, this chapter has emphasized the difference between parental alienation that was brought about by indoctrination and parental alienation without indoctrination. It is important to understand that distinction because the question of fault and responsibility may come up. That is, whose fault is it when parental alienation occurs? In the case of parental alienation through indoctrination, the outcome is the fault of the parent who did the brainwashing. In the case of parental alienation without indoctrination, the outcome is not the fault of either parent as an individual. In that circumstance, the alienation was caused by the battle that was fought by both parents, so that the child took cover by gravitating completely to one side and away from the other side.

However, family relationships are complex and in many cases the parental alienation is not simply the result of one extreme ("with indoctrination") or the other ("without indoctrination"). There is a continuum of cases between these two extremes, in which the alienation is the result of several factors meeting and interacting with each other.

In one case, for example, all three family members, the divorced parents and the fifteen-year-old daughter, contributed to a severe form of alienation. The girl lived with the mother, but she wanted to move to the father's household. After the judge granted her request, the girl was transferred to her father's custody and she never visited her mother again. The girl did not have much explanation for her refusal to visit her mother, other than a few remarks that seemed vague and illogical: "My Mom's hard to live with. My stepfather is overbearing. I never want to see them again.''

After an evaluation, it seemed that all three of the participants in this drama had important roles. The mother was a rigid, critical person who sometimes was unpleasant company—but her behavior was certainly not bad enough to justify the daughter's rejection. The father did say a few things to encourage the girl's dislike of the mother—but he did not indoctrinate her or interfere with the visitation. The girl herself contributed to the impasse—she had a narcissistic, self-indulgent personality style and she did not want to inconvenience herself by maintaining a relationship with her mother. The lesson here is that the father, mother, and daughter all contributed to the resulting parental alienation. It did not make sense for any of them to blame the others for what had happened, but they did anyway.

Consider Counseling

A child with parental alienation may be taken to a therapist. First of all, the mother (for instance) will explain to the therapist that the child absolutely refuses to visit the father. The mother will say that she has encouraged the child to visit many times, but she doesn't want to force the child to visit because he is likely to become hysterical and violent. Although the mother claims to want the child to have a good relationship with the father, she understands his reluctance because she knows that ''the father is a complete bum.'' When the child is interviewed, he is likely to say basically the same thing as the mother stated, but he is not simply parroting her. In fact, he really believes that the father is a bum and he can cite various injustices that occurred several years previously to prove his point. These injustices usually seem rather minor, compared to the total rejection of the father that followed from them.

It is very hard to treat children who manifest parental alienation. Some of these children have firmly made up their minds and it is not easy to help them understand something that does not make sense to them, that is, that it is really possible to love two parents who have been strongly fighting and hating each other. In therapy, it might be possible to help the child have a good relationship with both parents if the following conditions are met: that the parents have finally agreed to a lasting cease-fire; that both parents really support the notice that the child should have a good relationship with both of them; that all efforts to indoctrinate, whether blatant or subtle, cease; that the child is encouraged, usually by a competent therapist, to spend time with the rejected parent and see what happens; and that the child is innately strong enough and brave enough and flexible enough to reach out to the rejected parent.

It usually takes more than one therapist to deal with a case of parental alienation. Depending on the clinical circumstances, it might work for one therapist to see the child and a separate therapist to be the mediator for the parent. The best way to "treat" parental alienation is to not let it happen in the first place. The next chapter, "Living in Two Homes," gives more suggestions for how to help children have good relationships with both parents.

Chapter Seven
Living in Two Homes

Freddie had a complicated life for a boy in the fourth grade. His parents were divorced, so he lived with his mother and he had visitation with his father. His visitation schedule was not unusual for a child in elementary school, in that he stayed with his father every other weekend from Friday afternoon to Sunday evening. His father wanted to maximize their time together, so he arranged to pick Freddie up from school as soon as class ended on Friday afternoon. However, the father had a stubborn streak in him and felt that the mother, the custodial parent, should be in charge of Freddie's wardrobe. Since he paid child support to the mother, the father did not want to buy any additional clothes for Freddie and did not want to be responsible for washing clothes. The result was that Freddie had to take a small suitcase with him every Friday to school, so he would have clothes for the weekend. He and his mother had to make sure that he had play clothes for Saturday, church clothes for Sunday, and a couple of clean handkerchiefs. Since those clothes belonged to the mother, she always made sure when Freddie returned on Sunday that they all were returned to her. If one of those handkerchiefs were missing, there was hell to pay. Although Freddie enjoyed seeing his father, the visitation became a big headache for him. The visits always started off badly, because it was embarrassing and awkward to take that suitcase to school on those Friday mornings. The visits always ended badly, because his mom and dad argued when something was missing from the suitcase when he returned home.

Many divorced parents who are working hard to raise their children feel like they are reinventing the wheel. High schools and colleges do not teach how to raise children when the parents are divorced. It is unlikely that parents would know how to do it from their own past experience, so they end up using trial and error. The purpose of chapters seven, eight, nine, and ten is to give specific suggestions for dealing with common situations that occur when parents are divorced.

Helping the Child to Love Both Parents

Many children of divorced parents actually do have a comfortable, loving relationship with both the mother and the father. These children are lucky. Their parents are not doing anything particularly hard or unusual to bring this about. All they do is refer to the other parent in a neutral or positive tone, rather than with a voice dripping in criticism. They both try to make the visitation a positive experience, rather than a recurring dreaded event. If they have a disagreement, they work it out in some way that does not make the child a witness or an unwilling participant. A divorced parent may foster the child's affection for the other parent by helping the child make a simple Christmas present or helping him select an inexpensive card for Mother's Day or Father's Day.

What to Call the Stepparent

One of the things that divorced parents fuss about a lot is what name or term the child uses in referring to a stepparent. In my opinion, parents in both households make too big a deal out of this issue. That is, a man will remarry and will ask his son to refer to the stepmother as Mommy. The mother, of course, will find out about this and will go through the ceiling. She'll retaliate by insisting that the child never refer to the stepmother as Mommy in the mother's presence. The poor child may put a lot of energy into working out a system intended to keep everybody happy. In the father's household, he'll call the stepmother Mommy and his biological mother Mom. In the mother's household, he'll try to remember to refer to his stepmother as Bertha and call his mother Mommy. Undoubtedly the child will get confused and will sometimes refer to one or another of the adults by the wrong name.

There must be a solution to this common, vexing problem. The solution has two parts. The first part is to help the child find a name or term for the stepparent that he finds natural and comfortable. The child should not be pressured to call the stepparent Mom or Dad if it makes him feel funny. An informal poll has revealed that most

There are many stories about Mahatma Gandhi, who struggled for the independence of India and subsequently tried to reduce the strife between the Muslim and the Hindu peoples of this land. One time a man was very distraught and came to Gandhi for help. The man, who was a Hindu, was in a civil conflict and he killed a Muslim man. The Hindu was sad and upset because the Muslim's son was left an orphan. He asked Gandhi for forgiveness. Gandhi suggested that the Hindu adopt the child, which he agreed to do. Then Gandhi added that the Hindu man should devote his life to raising the boy to be a devout Muslim. It must evoke a similar feeling, when divorced parents are asked to help their children have a healthy and affectionate relationship with their former spouses.

children refer to their stepparents by their given names, such as George or Betty. If given permission to use the stepparent's first name, the child rapidly gets comfortable with it. Also, it makes it much easier to know whom he is talking about. The second part to the solution is to be completely tolerant when the child later gets the names mixed up and uses the wrong one. Every so often the child is going to refer to his mother as Betty and his stepmother as Mommy. Don't make it into a big deal. The child will usually correct himself and continue on with the conversation.

Continuity in Activities

There are many simple, practical things that parents can do that help children adjust to living in two households. To start with, it might help for the adult to put himself or herself in the child's place. For most adults, it would be really aggravating if every few days they had to change their phone number, their bed, their wardrobe, and their entire family. With a little extra effort, divorced parents can minimize the daily and weekly disruptions that their children experience.

Parents should figure out a way for their children to maintain friendships, extracurricular activities, and special interests, regardless of which household the child happens to be in. To be specific, it should be possible for a youngster to be on a soccer team and get to the practices and the games, no matter which parent he happens to be with at the time. It should be possible for the child to attend a classmate's birthday party, even if he is with the noncustodial parent that weekend. It should be possible for the child to be active in the Boy Scouts, even if he has visitation every other weekend. In fact, it might be a good idea for the noncustodial parent to volunteer as the assistant to the soccer coach or one of the leaders for the Tiger Cubs, since that would help the parent and the child have a regular activity together.

Spending the Night

A popular activity for children is spending the night with a friend. For some reason, noncustodial parents have the idea that children should never spend the night with a friend on the weekend when visitation occurs. Sometimes the noncustodial parent has the idea that visitation time should mean that he and the child are together and nobody else is around. It would seem more natural for the noncustodial parent and the child to try to enter each other's schedules, rather than trying to design "quality time" together.

For instance, suppose your child wants to have a friend sleep over on Saturday night, during a visitation weekend. Most child visitors don't need much space—they usually bring their own sleeping bags. The noncustodial parent might even want to include the visiting child's parents for a casual Saturday evening dinner or a simple Sunday morning brunch. The main point is that these are ways for the noncustodial parent to enter his child's world and to have a greater involvement in the child's day-to-day life. The purpose of visitation is to fulfill the child's needs, not the parent's.

Clothes and Toys

Is there some way that children like Freddie, who was mentioned at the beginning of this chapter, would not have to take a suitcase with him to school every Friday? The simplest solution would be for him to have a supply of everyday clothes in both of his homes. He should also have a supply of games, toys, and books in both homes. Ideally, a younger child would even have a teddy bear or a special blanket in both homes.

The way to make that happen is to allow the child to develop an attachment to two special blankets at the same time. On one of the visitations, he leaves one of the blankets at the noncustodial home, so he ends up with a transitional object in both places. By the way, some therapists will say this can't be done. They learned about the importance of transitional objects in graduate school and they have assumed that children can be attached to only one special object at a time. In some ways, however, children are more adaptable than we give them credit for.

What about presents? I think that there should be some coordination between divorced parents regarding major presents, such as expensive bicycles, watches, ski equipment, and so on. In many cases, the parent may want to select a present that relates to an activity that the parent and child enjoy together. Some divorced parents have major battles over whether a child will take a particular present with him to the other household. I think that the child should have personal possessions in both homes, and it generally works best if he leaves presents in the household where he received them. So the custodial parent will give the child a few Christmas presents, which stay in that home; the noncustodial parent will give the child a few presents, which will stay in that home. However, I don't think that parents should become fanatical about that issue. If you give your son a watch for his birthday, you should let him wear it to the other household—and you should accept the fact that he may lose it there!

Coordinating Discipline

Children and adolescents in intact homes are skillful at getting their way by manipulating their parents. I think that children take a course in kindergarten on how to identify the parent who is most likely to grant them a particular favor. When parents are divorced, manipulative children have a field day. Not only do the parents not communicate, but the parents and other relatives may feel sorry for the child and may be overly indulgent.

Many children are not consciously trying to work the parents against each other, but are merely trying to have their own needs met. Other children knowingly take advantage of their parents' divorce in order to achieve their own purposes. For example, a fifteen-year-old girl explained eloquently and somewhat guiltily how she used her parents' divorce for her own advantage. She knew that if she actively stirred up trouble between her parents, they would not be talking with each other and would not check out her stories with each other. She could then claim that her mother had given her permission to do something in order to influence her father, and vice versa.

Most children find that life is less confusing if the basic rules are consistent. Although divorced parents are not expected to agree on every aspect of raising their children, it is helpful if they coordinate the most common decisions that arise almost every day. For example: "Bedtime is 9:00 on school nights and 10:00 on weekends"; "You may go to PG-13 movies, but no R-rated movies"; "You had D's on your report card, so that means you cannot use the car until the next report card, if your grades are up." When it comes to discipline, the last thing Parent A should do is befriend the child by letting him get away with something that Parent B does not allow. Of course, life is not perfect and even parents in intact families may disagree on discipline and be inconsistent. I am simply suggesting that it is in the child's interests if divorced parents were to make some attempt at agreeing on the most common household rules.

Enjoying the Usual Routine

Sometimes noncustodial parents have felt that they needed to be superparents during every visit. They entertained their children intensively and planned extraordinary activities for each weekend they had together. I doubt that they had much fun.

It probably makes more sense to have a regular, rather predictable routine during visitation, such as: cooking a meal together; doing some errands or some chores together; doing something fun together, but it does not have to be anything elaborate. It sometimes works well for the parent and child to develop or expand on a common hobby or interest. It could be a hobby like photography or collecting bugs, that has a visible, tangible product. Or it could be an activity like hiking or tennis, that the child and parent enjoy doing together. In either case, the child and the noncustodial parent develop a sense of continuity by working on the same project or activity from week to week. When this process works, the child looks forward to the next visitation. There is more on the subject of visitation in the next chapter.

Chapter Eight
Making Visitation Work

Maggie Folsom, age nine, lived with her mother and had visitation with her father every other weekend and every Wednesday evening. Her mother was a nervous woman who was very concerned about Maggie and wanted to assure herself that Maggie was not having any problems when she was at her father's house. Therefore, Ms. Folsom started to telephone Maggie every weekend on Saturday morning, Saturday evening, and Sunday morning. These phone calls interrupted Maggie's activities, so the girl became abrupt and sounded irritated with her mother. Maggie tried to avoid the phone calls and made them as brief as she could. Ms. Folsom thought that Maggie was not acting like her usual self on the telephone, so she started worrying even more and questioned the girl in detail when she returned from the visitation. Since the phone calls and the interrogations made the visits unpleasant for Maggie, she started to say that she would rather not visit her father so frequently. Ms. Folsom became convinced that the father was neglecting or even abusing Maggie, so she petitioned the court to curtail his visitation.

Divorced parents put an enormous amount of energy into fussing and fuming about visitation. Just for starters, almost every custodial parent will be concerned that the visitation times interfere with or seriously compromise the child's usual activities. For instance, "Jimmy will be severely traumatized because he will be visiting his father in Cleveland instead of having ice cream at his best friend's birthday party." Almost every noncustodial parent will believe that the child's emotional and social and educational problems would be solved if only the visitations were longer and more frequent. Children feel miserable when their parents argue about the visitation schedule; about whether the child is ready on time, which is blamed on the custodial parent; about whether the child gets back on time, which is blamed on the noncustodial parent; and what actually happened during the visitation.

Typical Visitation Schedules

It is possible to state some general guidelines regarding visitation schedules that are related to the age of the child. Because of individual differences and special family circumstances, however, there are many reasons why divorced parents might work out a visitation schedule that differs from these guidelines. These suggestions are meant to be a starting point for more detailed discussions.

• *Very young children.* There may be some difference of opinion about what is the best living arrangement for very young children, up to age two. Some professionals would say that very young children need almost complete stability and need to sleep in the same bed in the same home every night. Others would say that very young children can easily handle multiple caretakers and certain kinds of change in their daily routine. There are thousands of young children in day care—these children spend about half of their waking hours during the course of the week at the day-care center and about half at home. With that in mind, wouldn't those same children be able to handle living about half the time with the mother and about half the time with the father?

Suppose the divorced couple agreed that the mother were to work and the father were to stay home for two years. In that case, the child could live with the father during the days and half of each weekend; the child could live with the mother every evening and the other half of the weekend. I think most people would agree, that if the mother were working full-time, it would be better for the child to stay with the father during the days than to be placed in a day-care center. The reverse arrangement would also apply, if the father worked and the mother stayed home for two years. In that case, the child could live with the mother during the days and half of each weekend; the child could live with the father every evening and the other half of the weekend.

Suppose both parents worked and the divorced couple hired a baby-sitter. The child could live in the mother's home for one week, with the baby-sitter supervising her during the day. The child could live with the father the next week, with the same baby-sitter during the days. The child would have the continuity of the baby-sitter and also have a relationship with both parents. These arrangements may seem unusual to some people, but they appear to work. The main point is that a young child can form

There are specific developmental tasks that children ordinarily accomplish in a step-by-step fashion as they get older. For example, there are physical tasks, such as learning to sit up, to crawl, to walk, and to run. There are also psychological tasks, and these tasks should be considered in devising visitation arrangements for children of different ages. The psychological task for very young children (up to age 2) is to develop a sense of trust in their primary caretakers. The psychological task for toddlers (about age 2 to 4) is the process of separation and individuation. That means that the child has a sense of his own individuality and he becomes comfortable with brief separations from primary caretakers. The task for preschoolers (about age 4 to 6) is to define themselves within the family, which usually takes the form of identifying with traits in the parents. The task for school children (about age 6 to 12) is to achieve a sense of self-worth through mastery of skills. The task for adolescents (about age 13-18) is to establish an identity separate from the parents.

attachments to several people (mother, father, baby-sitter, grandmother) and be comfortable with any of them.

If the young child, up to age two, is already quite comfortable with both mother and father, visitation could be practically any schedule. The arrangement could even be living half the time with each parent. The child should continue to be comfortable with both parents if both the custodial and the noncustodial parent see the child frequently and regularly.

But what if the young child is not familiar with or comfortable with the noncustodial parent? In that case, the goal of the visitation is for the child to become attached to the noncustodial parent, so they will be comfortable with each other. In general, that means starting with brief visitations, usually in the custodial parent's household, and then gradually increasing the child's exposure to the noncustodial parent. The visitations should be brief, but frequent. For example, they may be several times a week for two hours at a time. During those times the noncustodial parent should actually be in charge of the child, like a baby-sitter or a nanny. He would be there to feed the child, change the diaper, and perhaps put the child down for a nap, if that were the child's routine at the end of the visitation time.

Since the visitation with young children frequently takes place in the custodial parent's home, the question will arise as to what the custodial parent should do during that time. It would be best if she could keep out of the way, so that the child and the noncustodial parent could really feel like they were spending time together. If there has been a lot of conflict between the parents, it would be nice if the mother could be out of the home during the time of the father's visitation. Although it might be hard to make the arrangements, since it would mean having a neutral person stay in the home with the noncustodial parent, keeping the two parents away from each other might save wear and tear on everybody.

- *Pre-school children.* Children who are age two to five usually live primarily in one household and have visitation in the noncustodial parent's home. Although there is no exact formula for what visitation should be, a typical schedule might provide for two visits a week. For example, a four-year-old might visit the noncustodial parent every other weekend with one overnight, such as Saturday morning to Sunday afternoon. In addition, the child might see the noncustodial parent on one or two weekday evenings each week. To provide a second example following the same principle, the visitation could be every Tuesday evening for dinner and one overnight every weekend, from Friday evening to Saturday evening.

- *School-age children.* As children get older, the visitation usually is less frequent but longer in duration. For example, older children might visit the noncustodial parent every other weekend with two overnights, such as Friday evening to Sunday evening. In addition, they might see the noncustodial parent on one weekday evening each week. There is no rule that the visitation must follow that schedule, since it might be convenient to do it differently. For instance, there may be an advantage for some divorced parents to arrange visitation with the noncustodial parent to occur every weekend, from Saturday morning to Sunday evening, in order to have the child on a regular weekly schedule.

- *Adolescents.* When children enter high school, visitation becomes more individualized. Many youngsters continue to visit the noncustodial parent every other weekend, but the actual schedule becomes more variable because other activities are occurring in their lives. By this time the weekday evening visitations have usually ended.

In the stressful time following the divorce, it is helpful to have a definite visitation schedule that has been planned out months ahead of time. It usually works best for both parents to adhere to the schedule religiously. The reason for the strict schedule is that it gives the newly divorced parents one less thing to argue about. Also, it is extremely reassuring to the child to know that she will be seeing the noncustodial parent at a regular, predictable time each week. Once the dust settles, it might not be so necessary to stick to a rigid schedule. It may be a sign that divorced parents are getting more comfortable working out issues with each other, when they mutually agree to deviate from the schedule that had already been planned out.

Siblings

There is a tendency in these cases for parents and attorneys and judges and therapists to invent or develop very strict, rigid rules that they feel should be followed by all divorced families. One of the "rules" I have heard several times is that all of the siblings should have visitation at the same time. The judge may say, for instance, that the four minor children (ages 16, 10, 8, and 2) will live with the mother and will visit the father every other weekend. The judge literally means that all four children will visit the father, *en masse,* on every occasion that visitation occurs. To me, that does not make any sense at all.

When there are several children, visitation should be arranged in a way that maximizes the ability of the noncustodial parent to spend meaningful time with each child. If the children had different visitation schedules, the result would be that *both* parents would be able to spend time with the children individually. In the family with the four children, suppose the sixteen-year-old is a girl. Since her weekends are busy, she and her father agree that they will have dinner together every Wednesday evening. Let's suppose the ten-year-old and eight-year-old children are boys. The parents agree that they will visit the father together every other weekend, Friday evening to Sunday evening. And the two-year-old is a little girl. The dad sees her every Tuesday evening and every other weekend, Friday evening to Saturday afternoon. The younger girl and the two boys alternate, so that one weekend the father has the daughter and the next weekend he has the two boys together.

This father would need to keep his calendar organized, since he sees one or two of his children most of the days of every week. The reader should not go overboard and become rigid in the opposite direction. I am not suggesting that the four children in the example *never* visit the father together. There hopefully will be some occasions—for instance, a special picnic, a week of summer vacation—when the father and the four children would be together at the same time.

Transition Times

The most difficult time for young children is the transition from one household to another. It is disruptive; it means separation from a loving parent; it means an interruption in the day's activities; it means some inevitable tension, as the child's care is being passed from one parent to the other. The last thing the child needs is to witness hostility, sarcasm, and resentment.

Some parents, who get on each other's nerves, find it is better to structure the transition in such a way that the parents do not have to speak to each other. For instance, if the mother is picking the child up from the father's home, it is agreed that the mother will stay in her car and the father will stay on the porch, while the child walks out to the car to leave.

Another way to avoid parental conflict at the transition times is to arrange it so that the parents do not even see each other. If a young child is in day care, it might work smoothly for the father to pick the child up for weekend visitation on Friday afternoon and return the child to the day-care program on Monday morning.

If the transitions are not occurring smoothly, the parents may need to meet with a counselor or mediator to work out a pleasant way for the child to go from one household to the other. In extreme cases, the transitions may occur at the therapist's office. For instance, suppose there has been a great deal of conflict between the parents and the child has been caught up in it, so the entire divorced family is in counseling. The counselor could schedule the appointments for Friday afternoons. The mother brings the child to the appointment, and the counselor spends the first part of the meeting with the mother and child together, reviewing the plans for the visitation. Then the mother leaves. A little while later, the father arrives and that latter part of the therapy meeting is with the father and child together, in which they review again the plans for the visitation. At the end of the session, the child leaves with the father.

Consideration for the Child's Wishes

Divorced parents sometimes go to unusual extremes with their children. Some parents become overly indulgent. Others have a rejecting attitude toward this child, because they have transferred feelings from the ex-spouse to the child. Divorced parents may have a hard time figuring out how much to consider the child's preferences and demands, especially regarding visitation arrangements. In many situations it is helpful for the parents to think through whether it is best for the child to have very much say about the visitation schedule, before making the actual decision.

Parents can err by giving too much consideration to the child's stated preferences. For example, the custodial parent may announce that the child can visit the other parent whenever he wants. Or she may ask the child if he wants to visit the father this weekend or if he wants to stay home. That may seem like the mother is trying to be helpful to the child, but actually she is making it hard on him. Giving the child that much control over his visitation tends to put the child in the middle and intensifies his loyalty conflicts, because it is forcing the child to choose whether he wants to be with Mommy or Daddy. Some parents simply don't see that when they think they are doing something nice for the child, they are actually putting him in a meat grinder. Another time that a parent may be tempted to give the child's opinion too much consideration is when the child calls up and wants to be taken home. Ordinarily it is better for the child to continue the visitation until the end of the scheduled time.

Parents can err by giving too little consideration to the child's preferences. Parents should listen to the child's point of view, since they may get some good ideas. An example of giving too little consideration was the case of Merrie and Melodie at the beginning of chapter five. In that case the two parents had agreed on joint custody and arranged for their teenage daughters to alternate between the two households, one week at a time. The children simply wanted to live in one place and visit the other parent. The parents had been pretending to do what was the best interests of the children, to have continuing relationship with both of them, but were actually putting their own career needs above the children.

61

A general principle is that parents should give more consideration to the child's opinions and wishes as the child gets older. With younger children, it ordinarily works best for the adults to listen to the child's opinions, for the adults to make the decision, and then to stick to it. With older children and adolescents, it works better to have a greater amount of discussion and negotiation.

Giving Up Control

In divorced families, parents should expect that everyday events will not always go completely smoothly. As a result, no parent is going to be able to be in total control all the time. Parents have to give up the notion that the children are always going to be happy and comfortable. Growing up with divorced parents involves a certain amount of unhappiness, and there is no way to avoid it.

Giving up control means that the noncustodial parent will need to accept that the custodial parent will be making most of the decisions, especially those involving education and medical care and most day-to-day discipline.

Giving up control means that the custodial parent will not have complete knowledge or complete authority when the child is away. During that time the noncustodial parent will need to be responsible for the child's recreational activities, for his dinner, and for necessary medical care. In particular, parents like Ms. Folsom, at the beginning of this chapter, will need to let the child have her visitation without repeatedly intruding. Some parents may be a little anxious when the child is away for the weekend, but they need to learn patience and resolve the anxiety within themselves. These anxious parents benefit the children when they refrain from making overly frequent phone calls. If they don't hear from their mother every single day, these children are more likely to feel stronger and able to be more emotionally self-sufficient.

Chapter Nine
Holidays

Mr. Holmes called his attorney on Thursday afternoon in a complete tizzy. It had dawned on him that the following Sunday, three days off, was Father's Day. Although he had visitation with the children every other weekend, they were not scheduled to be with him that particular Sunday. He felt greatly aggrieved, because he remembered that the visitation schedule had resulted in the children spending Mother's Day with their mother. Mr. Holmes called his attorney, who called the mother's attorney, who called the mother, who said, "I'm terribly sorry, but the children and I have already made plans to go on a picnic on Sunday afternoon with family friends, so they will not be able to see their father that day." The mother's attorney called the father's attorney who called the father and said, "Too bad, but your ex-wife stubbornly refuses to let the children be with you on Father's Day." Mr. Holmes felt himself becoming furious and indignant. He went home early, skipped dinner, and put away four Scotch and waters, doubles.

Divorced parents and the judges who tell them how to organize their lives have found many different ways to deal with holidays and other special occasions. Sometimes the divorce decrees have very elaborate schedules that designate how the holidays will be spent for years to come. Most judges have the idea that the way to make important holidays equal for the two parents is to alternate them from year to year. In other words, the judge might say that this year the children will be with the father on Thanksgiving day until 4:00 P.M. and with the mother from 4:00 until 9:00 P.M.; with the father on Christmas Eve and until 8:00 A.M. on Christmas and then spend the rest of the day with the mother. And that next year will be the reverse of this year: the children will be with the mother on Thanksgiving day until 4:00 P.M. and with the father from 4:00 until 9:00 P.M.; with the mother on Christmas Eve and until 8:00 A.M. on Christmas and then spend the rest of the day with the father.

Parents and judges sometimes make detailed provisions for particular days that seem rather minor on the scale of events, such as Mother's Day, Father's Day, and each parent's birthday. In fact, some of these supposedly special occasions never received more than a fleeting notice by either the children or the parents until the custody and visitation negotiations got under way.

Another common error is the notion that the children should fully celebrate every important occasion with both of the divorced parents every year. It is not unusual, for instance, for children of divorced parents to be subjected to two complete Thanksgiving dinners; to be entertained by Santa in all his regalia in both households; and to celebrate each of their birthdays twice, complete with duplicate parties.

Self-Centered Parents

What is wrong with these complicated schedules and duplicated celebrations? The most important thing wrong with them is that the parents who devise them are working from an egocentric and perhaps a selfish point of view. The parent seems to be saying to herself, ''It is really important for my child to celebrate Thanksgiving with me and my relatives this year.'' The other parent is, of course, saying the same thing to himself, but neither one of them is correct. The parent doesn't realize that she is really defining what is important to herself, that is, that the child be with her on that special day. What actually is important to the child is to enjoy a day like Thanksgiving with one of his parents and perhaps with that parent's extended family or close friends. If it goes well, the child is going to feel about as thankful as he can get. Trying to squeeze in two Thanksgiving celebrations with two different families is simply going to make him feel rushed, used by both parents, and stuffed.

The people who devise the complicated schedules that alternate from year to year have the idea that it is important for the children of divorced parents to participate in the traditions of both the mother's household and the father's household. That certainly sounds right, and I'm not disagreeing with that basic premise. However, the judges and the attorneys who make up the schedules seem to have a very superficial notion as to how family traditions actually play themselves out. They seem to know that family traditions are going to be important for these children, even though their parents are divorced, but then they create schedules that are surely going to prevent the children from ever experiencing a true family tradition.

Importance of Tradition

What is a family tradition and why does it even matter? Most of the significant family traditions involve the merging of a specific event or day (such as Christmas; a wedding; the last two weeks of August at the beach) with the same set of people (close family friends, grandparents, other extended family) and with something that involves family values (the religious implications of Hanukkah and Christmas, the patriotic aspect of the Memorial Day parade, the romantic aspect of a wedding). A child who grows up in an intact family in which traditions are consistently observed starts to blend together the feelings that are associated with the event, the people involved, and the values. If the occasions are reasonably pleasant and happy, the child would be more likely to assimilate the values that are associated with the event.

For the child to benefit from family traditions, the experience must be administered in a consistent manner, on a regular schedule, and in the right dose. Ideally, the child would have the same basic experience with the same set of important people (relatives and close family friends) year after year. I doubt that a child, whose parents are divorced, would incorporate anything very useful from holidays that were marked by hustling from one household to another, by arguments over the exact schedule for the day, and by cursory contacts with both sets of grandparents. The challenge for divorced parents is to find a way to help the children experience a strong sense of family tradition, even though they are growing up in two different households.

Dividing the Holidays

I have a specific suggestion for how divorced parents should deal with holidays. My approach is intended to maximize the children's sense of being truly involved in family traditions, rather than being part-time players in other people's holidays. What I recommend is that the parents make a list of all the holidays that they consider really meaningful. Then they divide up the holidays in a way that is equitable. The plan is that the division that is established would continue indefinitely. In other words: (1) the child would only be in one household for any particular special day and (2) the child will be in the same household for that day every year.

For instance, two divorcing parents made this list of the days that they considered meaningful:

Christmas Eve
Christmas Day
Thanksgiving Day
Friday after Thanksgiving
Memorial Day weekend
Labor Day weekend
New Year's Day
Fourth of July

In this system it usually works out best to divide up the really big occasions into two parts, such as: Christmas Eve and Christmas Day; Thanksgiving Day and the Friday after Thanksgiving. Since there were eight meaningful days for these parents, they divided them up so that each parent had four. The father ended up with Christmas Eve, Thanksgiving Day, New Year's Day, and Memorial Day weekend. That means that he will always have the children on Christmas Eve, year in and year out. It means that he can construct his own consistent tradition for his children for that day. The children will grow up feeling that Christmas Eve has a warm, consistent, and predictable feeling to it. In this particular case, the mother ended up with Christmas Day; the Friday after Thanksgiving; the Fourth of July; and Labor Day weekend. She will feel good because she and her children will consistently be able to attend her family's traditional picnic on the Fourth of July. Her children will grow up feeling that they are an important part of that Fourth of July softball game because they are there every single year.

This method of dividing the holidays works well when the list consists of about eight or ten special days during the year. This method does not work well if it is pushed to include more and more days, because then it starts to disrupt the basic visitation schedule that itself is supposed to be predictable for the children.

There may be many special days that deserve some degree of recognition, but do not really need to be celebrated exactly on the right date. I would put Mother's Day, Father's Day, and the parents' own birthdays in that category. For instance, I think it is a good idea for the child to recognize Father's Day and his father's birthday with a card, a small present that he made himself, and perhaps a phone call if he happens to be in his mother's household that day. But it does not need to be much more than that and the child does not actually need to be with the father on that day.

In an intact home, the celebration of the father's birthday and of Father's Day is usually instigated by the mother, not by the children. In a divorced family, the mother will usually need to remind a young child that Father's Day is coming up and the mother might even need to help the child prepare a card for her former husband.

Some divorcing couples may feel strongly that Mother's Day and Father's Day and perhaps other days should be considered important enough to be on the list of special days to be officially divided. That's fine, since different families are going to have their own interests and values. In general, however, divorced parents should try to agree on using holidays to create a sense of family traditions for the children. What that means is that parents should try to think about the meaning of the holiday and the actual experience of the day from the child's point of view, and not simply to consider their own priorities.

Chapter Ten
Noncustodial Parents

Andy, age fourteen, was visiting his noncustodial father for the weekend. After they watched "Saturday Night Live" together, Andy tripped on a rug, fell down, and cut his leg. The father took his son to the local emergency room late at night, where Andy's laceration was sutured. When Andy went home the next day, his mother learned of the injury and its treatment. It was basically a happy ending: the noncustodial father felt that he had been a good parent; Andy felt that he had a good dad; and the mother was relieved that she had not been called to the emergency room the night before. This kind of event is a commonplace occurrence, but it has a serious flaw. According to some legal authorities, the noncustodial father did not have the right to authorize the treatment; the hospital did not have the right to accept Andy as a patient; and the physician who put in the sutures could be charged with assault and battery.

Since the relationship between divorced parents is often contentious, children suffer when they are victims of the ongoing dispute over both big and little issues. One issue that creates a great deal of misunderstanding and anger is defining the relative rights of the custodial and the noncustodial parents. There is disagreement regarding this particular issue among professionals who work with divorced parents. There is a big difference between what is stated theoretically—for instance, the strict legal definition of the rights of noncustodial parents—and what happens in everyday practice.

There needs to be a framework for defining the relative rights of custodial and noncustodial parents. The purpose of creating consistent standards and guidelines is quite simple. That is, divorced parents are more likely to become angry and to fight over the child when there is ambiguity in their relationship. What we lack in our society are basic, generally accepted ground rules for the most common postdivorce situation, when one parent has custody of the child and the other one does not. We need to develop guidelines that divorced parents, attorneys, judges, and therapists can apply in a consistent manner. If the rules of the game were more definite, each parent would have clearer expectations and would be less likely to feel cheated and resentful when he doesn't get what he was hoping for.

Some authorities say that defining the rights of the noncustodial parent is an unnecessary exercise. They say that divorced parents are going to fight about something and if it turns out they cannot fight about the noncustodial parent's rights, they will find some other battleground. I am not that pessimistic, although I do think that divorced parents need all the help they can get if they are going to cooperate in raising their children. One way to help these parents is to provide structure, to lay out clearly each parent's rights and responsibilities.

Bringing some resolution to this issue would help therapists and medical personnel. If there were standardization regarding the rights of the custodial and noncustodial parents, it would help to structure and organize some aspects of divorce mediation, custody and visitation evaluations, counseling for divorcing parents, and the therapy for their children. I am saying that it would be better if every divorcing couple did not have to reinvent the wheel, when it comes to defining the noncustodial parent's role in the child's life.

In this chapter "she" will be used to refer to the custodial parent and "he" to the noncustodial parent. I am following that convention simply for clarity and for easy reading. There is no implication that the mother is more suited or more likely to be the custodial parent.

Legal Opinions

Existing state laws and the higher courts have provided few guideposts regarding the rights of the noncustodial parent. Several legal precedents can be cited, but there is no comprehensive definition of the relative rights of custodial and noncustodial parents. A state law may simply indicate that the custodial parent has responsibility for the child and thereby suggest that the noncustodial parent has no more rights regarding the child than a total stranger. These laws could lead one to believe that the noncustodial parent may not take the child for medical treatment, unless it is a true emergency and the custodial parent cannot be located. Of course, in a true emergency, any person on the street could take the child to a hospital and seek treatment. Some states do define in their laws specific rights for the noncustodial parent. For instance, there may be a law that provides that the noncustodial parent has a right to a copy of the child's medical records and to a copy of the child's report card.

In 1986 a court of appeals in Virginia addressed the question of how much latitude a noncustodial parent should have during visitation. The court said that the noncustodial parent could provide whatever recreation he desired for the child, as long as it was not clearly dangerous: ". . . absent a finding by the court that the noncustodial parent has acted without concern for the child's well-being or best interest, has demonstrated irresponsible conduct, has interfered with basic decisions in areas which are the responsibility of the custodial parent, or finding that the activity which is questioned by the custodial parent presents a danger to the child's safety or well-being, neither the custodial parent nor the court may intervene to restrict activities during visitation." In that particular opinion, the court permitted the noncustodial parent to allow his child to ride a motorized dirt bike on the family farm, although the custodial parent disapproved.

It is my impression that attorneys give inconsistent advice regarding the rights of the noncustodial parent, because it depends on who the client is. I think that the attorneys' inconsistencies are a natural consequence of dealing in an adversarial setting with an issue that has no firm guidelines. It seems to me that the attorney for the noncustodial father tells him that he should take whatever prerogatives he can get away with, especially if the particular issue had not been spelled out explicitly in the divorce agreement. The attorney for the custodial parent tells her that she may have the right to limit the father's access to the child's school, pediatrician, therapist, and so on.

Physicians hear one thing from attorneys and something else from professional colleagues. Attorneys usually advise physicians to take whatever steps are necessary to guard against the remote possibility of some future lawsuit. Many attorneys would recommend that the doctor not treat a child without the permission of the custodial parent because there is some infinitesimal possibility he might be sued for assault and battery. However, that is not what happens in practice. It is common for family practitioners and for pediatricians to treat children at the request of noncustodial parents, stepparents, grandparents, and even baby-sitters.

General Principles

The way I address this problem is to start with a fundamental principle. That is, it is usually in the child's best interests to feel that both of his parents love him and provide for him and take responsibility for him. That means that the noncustodial parent should be fully responsible when this child is in his charge.

The noncustodial parent has greater rights than a baby-sitter or a full-time nanny or the child's teacher. We need a systematic way to delineate the following gradation of authority over children:

- The custodial parent has ultimate and absolute responsibility for and authority over her child.
- The noncustodial parent has absolute responsibility for and authority over the child regarding most routine, day-to-day matters when the child is in his charge.
- Other individuals, such as baby-sitters and teachers, have more limited responsibility and more circumscribed authority over children in their charge.
- Total strangers have no responsibility or definite authority regarding other people's children, but they may choose to exercise limited authority in certain circumstances.

Recommended Guidelines

In this chapter I translate these basic principles into practical guidelines. The guidelines are not intended to be the last word in this discussion, but can be seen as an outline to be used by divorced parents, attorneys, judges, and therapists. These suggestions are not intended to advocate for any particular agenda, but hopefully reflect a balance between the interests of the child (to have a loving relationship with both parents . . .), the right of the custodial parent (to have ultimate responsibility for the child . . .), and the right of the noncustodial parent (to have substantial but somewhat limited responsibility for the child . . .).

These guidelines are intended to take a common sense approach to this question: How can two parents who may greatly disagree with each other cooperate in raising a child? In developing these guidelines, I am assuming that we are dealing with two responsible and capable and nurturing parents. I am addressing the extremely common situation in which both parents are adequate, but one of them happens to have legal custody of the child.

Extended Family

It is usually in the child's interests to maintain a good relationship with grandparents, other extended family members, and even the family friends of both parents. The implication here is that the custodial parent should not try to control the company that the noncustodial parent may keep during visitation.

Education

The custodial parent has the right to make the major decisions regarding the child's education, such as where he attends school and whether to authorize special education placement. It is usually wise for the custodial parent to consult the noncustodial parent in these decisions. The topic of ''Schools and Teachers'' is discussed in chapter twelve.

Religion

Several courts have ruled that both parents have the right to take the child to church and enroll the child in religious education. One would think that two reasonable parents would not subject a child to two totally different religious and philosophical points of view—but it happens and it is not unusual to see children who have been inculcated with some combination of Protestant or Catholic or Jewish ideology. I do not see any easy solution to this problem. One might predict that as adolescents these children will have great difficulty establishing a sense of identity and will become unusually cynical about religious issues.

Recreation

In the best of worlds, the custodial and noncustodial parents will cooperate in promoting the child's extracurricular and recreational activities. For instance, the parents may end up alternating in taking the child to soccer games. On the other hand, it should be understood that the noncustodial parent has the right to provide his choice of recreation for the child, as long as it is not dangerous. Since our society offers a wide range of recreational activities and since people have such individual tastes, the custodial parent frequently feels like criticizing the noncustodial parent's choice. Usually, the solution to this problem is that the custodial parent needs to give up some control and needs to accept that life does present risks, that the child may get scratched up if he goes body-surfing or may get blisters if he goes on a long hike. When the child visits the noncustodial parent for an extended time over the summer, the noncustodial parent should have the right on his own authority to enroll the child in a day camp or even an overnight camp.

Emergency Medical Care

One thing that attorneys, doctors, parents, and judges agree on is that noncustodial parents can take a child for emergency medical care. Of course, anybody at all can take a child for treatment of a true emergency, so that is no big deal.

Routine Medical Care

This is an area of confusion. Laws generally state that the custodial parent is responsible for medical care; purists interpret these laws to mean that the noncustodial parent has no authority at all in this area; but the common medical practice is to treat children at the request of noncustodial parents.

I think that the noncustodial parent should have complete responsibility for the child when he physically has the child with him. That means that the noncustodial parent should be encouraged to provide basic medical care at home when the illness is minor and to take the child to the pediatrician when the illness is more serious. The noncustodial parent should be able to authorize routine and reasonable tests, such as eye examinations, speech and hearing evaluations, X-rays, and laboratory tests. If the noncustodial parent is sending the child to camp for the summer, that parent should be able to arrange for the precamp physical examination and to authorize medical care at the camp. The reason for this recommendation is that it is good for the child to feel that the noncustodial parent is a complete parent, as much as possible. It is also more fulfilling for the noncustodial parent to actually be in charge when the child is in his care. Finally, it would really seem silly to require the physician in the situation regarding Andy, at the beginning of this chapter, to telephone Andy's mother to get permission to suture the boy's laceration.

Serious Nonemergency Medical Care

The custodial parent alone should have the authority to make major medical decisions, including hospitalization, surgery, and invasive procedures. I am suggesting, for instance, that a noncustodial parent might discover during the summer that his teenage daughter has scoliosis and could even take her to an orthopedic surgeon for a consultation and X-rays. However, it would be up to the custodial parent to authorize surgery.

Psychotherapy and Counseling

Psychiatric treatment, psychotherapy, and counseling are other kinds of "serious nonemergency medical care," that should only be authorized by the custodial parent. A noncustodial parent might have the idea that his child has attention-deficit/hyperactivity disorder, but it would be up to the custodial parent to decide whether to initiate a trial of medication. Absent an emergency, it is up to the custodial parent to authorize psychotherapy or counseling for the child.

Psychiatric and Psychological Evaluation

Most authorities say that the noncustodial parent should not be allowed to take a child for any kind of psychological or psychiatric evaluation, unless it is an emergency. Accepting these guidelines does create a lack of symmetry, in that the noncustodial parent could take the child for routine medical care but not for routine psychiatric care. The reason for taking this position is the suspicion that the noncustodial parent is consulting the psychiatrist simply to collect evidence for a lawsuit to gain custody of the child. It is considered unethical for mental health professionals to see the child in those circumstances because it only encourages the noncustodial parent to shop around and arrange repeated evaluations until he finds a therapist who says what he wants to hear.

The De Facto Custodian

In some situations, the legal custodian has been out of the picture for a very long time and the child is actually being raised by the noncustodial parent. In such a situation, the noncustodial parent should be allowed to make any and all decisions regarding the child.

Common Sense

We live in a very bureaucratic society and children of divorce are greatly victimized by legalistic wrangling, arbitrary rules, unrealistic and unnatural schedules, and other people's agendas. Divorced parents, physicians, and therapists need to find ways to do what makes sense for the child and not get hung up on the extremely remote prospect of being sued or criticized.

In the case of Andy at the beginning of this chapter, I would say that it made sense for the emergency room physician to suture the laceration and not worry about calling the custodial parent to obtain permission for this routine nonemergency procedure.

Custodial and noncustodial parents need to share parenting responsibilities in a way that makes sense to the child. I am taking that to mean that the custodial parent should have the final word regarding major educational and medical and other decisions. But the noncustodial parent should be fully responsible when the child is actually with him, which may include making many routine educational and medical and other decisions. The children of divorced parents will experience less confusion in their lives if our society develops a greater degree of standardization in the way custodial and noncustodial parents share their responsibilities.

Chapter Eleven
Stepfamilies and Blended Families

Sally and her mother and stepfather moved from Los Angeles to Boston. The explanation for this major relocation that was given to the general public was that the stepfather was offered an attractive job opportunity in Boston. The real reason was that the family wanted to get away from Sally's biological father in L.A. The father was an offensive alcoholic who had been physically abusive to the mother and who continued to harass her long after their divorce. The father was a showy, flamboyant man who worked on the fringes of the motion picture industry.

In Boston, Sally had two boyfriends. The first one was the bass guitarist of a rock band who had selected Sally to be his girl. The boyfriend dominated the relationship and took advantage of Sally both physically and psychologically. When they dated, Sally had to drive because his license had been suspended after driving while intoxicated. Sally enjoyed being the girlfriend of a local rock star, but she disliked the boyfriend's drinking and his behavior and his control over her. Sally gave the musician boyfriend an ultimatum to stop drinking, broke up with him, got back together again, and eventually broke up for good.

The second boyfriend in Boston was a classmate in her high school. He was polite, kind, good-looking, and rich. He seemed too good to be true. The moral of this story is that children and adolescents are greatly influenced by the personalities and the events in their nuclear families and also in their stepfamilies. Sally's relationships with her first boyfriend and the second boyfriend were echoes of the mother's relationships with the father and the stepfather. Perhaps Sally learned something from her mother's experience, that it is possible to have a satisfying, nonabusive relationship with a guy.

Stepfamilies or remarried families come about in three ways. Nowadays, the most common stepfamily history is that two parents divorced and then one or both of them remarried. Each time one of the parents remarries, a stepfamily is created. It does not matter whether the child is actually living with that particular parent. If both parents have remarried, the child is part of two stepfamilies: one stepfamily includes his mother, his stepfather, and himself; the second stepfamily includes his father, his stepmother, and himself. The second way to create a stepfamily is that a parent has died and the surviving parent remarried. A third possibility is that an unmarried mother might later marry a man other than the child's father.

In any case, stepfamilies have certain characteristics: the family members have experienced an important loss (of the former parent), whether through divorce or death; there is a new person in the household (the stepparent), who does not necessarily fit in perfectly well; from the child's point of view, there is a "missing" biological parent who is somewhere else; and the child may belong to two households with conflicting messages and values.

A blended family is a kind of stepfamily that is more complicated. For instance, two divorced parents may marry, both of whom already have children. You end up with both of the adults being a parent (to his or her own child) and a stepparent (to the spouse's child). Another way to create a blended family is for the parents of a stepfamily to have another child together. In that case, one child in the family still has a stepparent, while the other child has two biological parents in the same family. To add to the confusion, some people use inconsistent terminology and mix up stepfamilies with adoptive families and foster families.

Literary Allusions

Stepparents have not fared well in popular culture. The classic example was Cinderella's stepmother, who unfairly favored her own daughters over Cinderella. Of course, she ultimately got her comeuppance. Another example was a movie several years ago, *The Stepfather*, in which a man methodically and repeatedly married women who already had children. After an initial period of apparent stepfamily bliss, he would violently kill the woman and his stepchildren. He got his comeuppance also when one of the stepdaughters did him in.

Real life is not that dramatic. It does happen, however, that the child's relationship with the stepparent may affect and interfere with her

Dr. Emily Visher and Dr. John Visher have collected a good deal of information about stepfamilies, which has been based on their own personal experience, their clinical experience as a psychologist and a psychiatrist, and their study of available research. They wrote an important book together, *Stepfamilies: A Guide to Working with Stepparents and Stepchildren* (New York: Brunner/Mazel, 1979). Another resource for therapists is a book by William Hodges, *Interventions for Children of Divorce: Custody, Access, and Psychotherapy* (New York: John Wiley, 1986).

relationship with her parent. For instance, there was a girl named Lorrie, whose parents divorced and both of them remarried. Lorrie had a very problematic relationship with her stepmother, who was rejecting and almost abusive. For example, she criticized the father when he bought Lorrie a small gift. The stepmother browbeat Lorrie to the point that the two of them were not allowed to be home together without another person present. Although the girl previously had affection for her father, the continuing conflict with her stepmother eventually poisoned the relationship between Lorrie and her father. On the other hand, Lorrie got along perfectly well with her mother and her new stepfather.

Free Advice

Stepparents get a lot of advice, much of it unsolicited, on how to get along with the new stepchildren. The children's natural parent usually has some ideas about how they should deal with the stepparent. Sometimes grandparents, other relatives, and various friends get in the act. Not to be outdone, I wish to offer some suggestions to the parents of stepfamilies and blended families.

• Think about why you got married this time—because you wanted a long-term relationship with a new spouse. If you truly love each other, you will find ways to accommodate to each other's children.
• Feel good about just being yourself. Don't try to replace or make up for or be better than some previous parent. Be careful to not take on too much responsibility, such as trying to be superstepparent and doing all the jobs that belong to the parents.

- Don't force yourself into a place in the child's heart when that spot is already occupied. For instance, don't insist that the child call you Mom if the child already has a Mom. In fact, a good stepparent is usually comfortable with encouraging the child to relate to and respect the natural parent.

- Take you time to find out how you can best fit into the child's world. There will be important ways for you to shape the child's future, but you need to take some time to figure them out.

- On the other hand, be prepared to assume a role that is very meaningful for the child. A twelve-year-old boy who has no father at all is going to have high hopes if a new stepfather arrives.

- Put time and energy into building the foundation of a good relationship. Offer sincere compliments and show your appreciation to your stepchild. Arrange to do errands, activities, and fun events that just involve you and the stepchild. The stepparent and the child might try to identify or develop a common interest, which is a little special or a little different from their activities with other family members. Perhaps they both like science fiction or they both like taking care of the dog.

- In a blended family, the parents need to think through how they will parent together. They should actively encourage each child to have a good relationship with both his parent and his stepparent. They should sit down and talk about issues such as schools, financial priorities, and discipline.

- Stepfamilies and blended families need to be unusually clear about communication. Don't take things for granted. Talk it out. Have family meetings.

- In blended families, watch to make sure that the children really are being treated fairly and more or less equally. They are going to be sensitive to discrepancies. That does not mean that parents and grandparents need to calculate the value of presents down to the last nickel, to make sure that each child gets exactly the same. What it might mean at Christmas, for instance, is that the children get the same number of "big presents" and "little presents."

- In your new family, it is important to establish your own routines, rituals, and family traditions. See chapter nine, "Holidays."

- Feel that you are a family, for better or for worse. When problems arise, look for solutions within the family. Don't jump to the conclusion that the solution is to extrude one of the children.

• Adolescents raise particular problems. Teenagers come and go, so they are not consistent members of the blended families. They will have a developmental need to become physically and psychologically independent, which may be contrary to the blended family's need for cohesion.

Recycling

Being part of a blended family is a great opportunity to recycle and perhaps improve upon earlier relationships. If your first marriage was problematic, here's a chance to build a relationship on a firmer foundation. If you "blew it" when you raised your own children, perhaps you learned something, and will fare better with your stepchildren. Orchestrating a stepfamily or a blended family can be a tremendously satisfying experience for the parent, the stepparent, and the children. If you do not believe me, just watch some reruns of "The Brady Bunch."

Chapter Twelve
Schools and Teachers

Billie Jean, age three, was enrolled in the Happy Hours Preschool when her parents separated and started the process of divorcing. A custody dispute ensued and the temporary arrangement was for Billie Jean to live alternating weeks with her mother and her father. Both of the parents liked the Happy Hours Preschool and it was good that Billie Jean could continue there, since at least that part of the day had a sense of stability to it. Billie Jean's teacher, Ms. Edmondson, tried to stay in touch with both of the parents.

Ms. Edmondson noticed that Billie Jean was quite different each week and it seemed to be related to which parent she was living with at the time. When she was living with her mother, Billie Jean was more likely to seem irritable, manipulative, and overly demanding. When she was living with her father, Billie Jean was more pleasant and simply blended in better with the other children. What struck Ms. Edmondson the most was how differently her parents behaved and how Billie Jean related to her mother and father, when the parent dropped her off in the morning.

Billie Jean's mother followed an unpredictable schedule and dropped the girl off at a different time each day. The mother frequently seemed harried and disorganized. On one occasion the mother was wearing nightclothes and bathrobe when she delivered Billie Jean to nursery school. But what was most striking was that the mother made a very big production out of the simple process of dropping off her daughter. She hugged Billie Jean many times, gave her many reassurances, and usually had many instructions for Ms. Edmondson. The result was that Billie Jean always became emotionally upset at the separations from her mother, so the mother had to hug her a few more times. Ms. Edmondson also noticed that at the end of the day when the mother came to pick up Billie Jean, the girl was almost indifferent and seemed more interested in continuing some play activity rather than going home.

Ms. Edmondson observed a different pattern when Billie Jean's father dropped the girl off. The father came at the same time every day, gave Billie Jean a hug, said good-bye, and left. Billie Jean was not upset, but readily got involved with the activities at the preschool. At the end of the day, Billie Jean ran to greet her father and was eager to go home with him. Ms. Edmondson had several conversations with the father, and thought that he was very interested in comparing notes regarding play activities for young children, discipline, and other aspects of parenting.

When the custody dispute eventually came to court, both the mother and the father wanted Ms. Edmondson and other personnel from Happy Hours Preschool to testify. Ms. Edmondson preferred to keep out of the parental conflict, since she wanted to stay on good terms with both of the parents. She ultimately did testify, but did it in a way that seemed comfortable for her. That is, the teacher simply testified about the things that she had observed, the repetitive behavior patterns of the mother, the father, and of Billie Jean. Ms. Edmondson did not draw any conclusions about who the better parent might be and did not have any suggestions or recommendations to make. She merely described what she had seen. The judge took Ms. Edmondson's observations into consideration, along with much additional information, and ruled that the father should have custody of Billie Jean.

Since school is such an important part of the lives of all children, it is easy to see how teachers and school administrators are likely be very aware of the experiences of children of divorced parents. Teachers are in a wonderful position to be helpful to these children, although that may seem to go beyond their basic job description. Teachers, guidance counselors, and principals relate to children of divorce in many ways: as part of the support network for children of divorce; communicating with two sets of parents in different households and perhaps different communities; coping with two parents, who might be quite hostile to each other; and perhaps dealing with subpoenas and other legal issues.

School as Support Network

School is an important part of the support system for children of divorce because sometimes school is the only calm, predictable, sensible, and pleasant place for the child to be. Teachers can be helpful in many ways. For example, if a child seems unusually upset, the teacher might try to be reassuring and check with the youngster privately to see if he wants to talk about something. At some point it might be helpful to let the child know that it is fine to talk in classroom discussions about divorce, arguments, stepparents, and similar subjects. That does not mean that the teacher is trying to do psychotherapy. It only means that the teacher is communicating that it is fine to talk about subjects that seem touchy and sensitive—because many other children have had the same experience and it is useful for the child to discover that.

Teachers can also be helpful by letting children know, during the normal course of classroom activities, that there are many kinds of families. Some children have two parents; some have one parent; some have a stepparent; some are raised by grandparents. The point is that all of these families are fine and that children do not need to assume that the only right way to grow up is to have two parents in the same household. I am not suggesting that the teacher should give a lecture on this subject. On the contrary, there are many opportunities during everyday classroom activities to express this message.

For example, young children frequently draw pictures of their family members, either spontaneously or at the suggestion of the teacher. The pictures may provide a wonderful opportunity for the teacher to compliment the children's artistic abilities, but also to help them express the relationships of the people in their family and to understand that there are many acceptable ways to organize people in a household. Another opportunity may arise when the children hear a story in school about a family that is divorced. While respecting their right to privacy, the teacher might ask if there are any children in the classroom who live with a stepparent or a foster parent or whatever. The children might find it helpful to compare their own experiences with the characters in the story.

In order for the teacher to be helpful, she needs to know what is happening in the child's life. For younger children I think it is a good idea for parents to let the teacher know if something unusual has happened in the family. That includes items such as parental separation or divorce, the death of a grandparent, and the serious illness of a sibling. This knowledge allows the teacher to be sensitive and to understand why a child is behaving in a particular way. With that understanding, the teacher does a better job at teaching.

In many elementary schools, the guidance counselors are very much aware of the family arrangements of the children under their purview.

Some school counselors have found it helpful to have group meetings for children of divorce. The counselor would check first with the parent, of course, before including a child in such a group. These counseling groups are probably helpful because the child learns that other youngsters have had similar experiences. Some of these group counseling meetings consist of open-ended discussions; some involve the children relating events that happened at home; in some meetings the children might draw pictures of family members engaged in happy or not-so-happy activities; and in some meetings the counselor would give direct advice. For example, the counselor might encourage the children to try to stay out of conflict between the parents. If it seems possible to achieve, the counselor might encourage the children to try to have a satisfying and affectionate relationship with both parents.

Communication with Parents

In chapter ten, I explained how both the custodial and the noncustodial parent should be actively involved in the day-to-day work of child-rearing, not just in arranging for quality time. How should that general principle apply to the child's education? I think that both parents should be aware of educational issues, should meet the teachers, should be fully informed about the child's progress, and should go to PTA meetings. However, the custodial parent will be ultimately in charge, usually. If the parents can't agree, the custodial parent will make the decision that the child will attend School A rather than School B, will decide whether the child takes a sandwich or buys lunch in the cafeteria, and will authorize for the youngster to be in special education, if that happens to become necessary.

Since both parents should be involved as much as possible in educational issues, school administrators need to go to a lot of extra effort these days. When the child is registered at the beginning of each school year, the school office should collect accurate information regarding the following:

Whom does the child live with?
Who has custody?
Names, address, and phone numbers of mother and stepfather.
Names, address, and phone numbers of father and stepmother.

84

Who should receive report cards?

Who should receive other notices and school newsletters?

Who will be the primary contact person with the teachers?

Who is authorized to pick the child up from school?

Who should be called if the child is sick?

. . . and the experienced school administrator can probably think of a few more questions that are good to ask. Basically, it is useful to clarify the ground rules at the beginning of the year rather than several months later when the paternal grandmother suddenly shows up in the middle of the day to pick the child up.

It is my opinion that the child's school should send identical correspondence to the custodial parent and the noncustodial parent, which includes report cards, announcements of meetings, and school newsletters. The custodial parent should take care of the day-to-day communication with the child's teacher, but the noncustodial parent should have the opportunity once or twice during the school year to meet with the teacher.

I am sure that the suggestions in this chapter are not practiced everywhere. Educational policies and procedures are determined, at least in part, by state law, so the usual practice may be quite different from state to state. For example, in Tennessee there is a state law that says noncustodial parents have access to the educational records of their children. As a result, most schools in Tennessee automatically send report cards and other information to both parents. On the other hand, I'm told that the practice in Oklahoma is almost the opposite. That is, schools do not send anything to the noncustodial parent, unless the divorce decree spells out that school information should be sent to both parents.

Playing Referee

Just as a child may be caught in the middle between two battling parents, the child's teacher may be in the same spot. That is, the divorced parents may both try to win the alliance and the loyalty of the teacher. Both parents may be very demanding and try to talk the teacher into accepting their respective arguments. They may insist on completely contradictory agendas for the child. They may resent the fact that the teacher has had communication with the other parent. What should the beleaguered teacher do?

- Oftentimes, the teacher should follow the same advice that is given to the child, which is to stay out of the fighting. When the mother starts to complain about what an imbecile the father has been, the teacher can directly say that she is not interested in getting involved in that aspect of the child's life.
- If there is any confusion about the issue, the teacher should be clear about which parent to contact regarding everyday situations. If Jimmy has not done his homework, she should ordinarily touch base with the custodial parent, who has responsibility for sorting out routine educational issues. It is too much to expect the teacher to notify both parents about every little thing that happens in the classroom.
- However, it does make sense to have a system of notifying both parents about many events that happen at school: the periodic parent-teacher conferences; the class play; the holiday musical. The implication is that the teacher will have to develop a more elaborate communication system than simply sending a note home with Jimmy. She will need to have a mailing list for the parents of all her students. Some of those letters can go home with the students. Other letters will be mailed, such as the ones to the noncustodial parents.
- The teacher should figure out the method that works best for her regarding the parent-teacher conferences. It is my impression that most of the time, when parents are divorced, it is best to try to meet with both of the parents at the same time. That obviously saves the teacher some time and it makes it possible to make the same statement to both parents at the same time, which reduces possible misinterpretations and miscommunications.
- On the other hand, sometimes divorced parents are so angry at each other that it is pointless to have them in the same room at the same time. There is so much hostility that the teacher will not be able to accomplish anything with either of them. In such a case, it becomes necessary for the teacher to schedule separate parent-teacher meetings.
- What about important meetings that only happen once? An example would be the meeting with special education personnel to discuss an individual educational plan. It is important for the person organizing the meeting to make sure that the parent will be there who has the authority to make decisions regarding educational issues. It is usually helpful for the second parent to be present also, as long as the meeting does not turn into an argument between the two of them.

• What about the attendance at school events, such as the class play? Should both parents attend these occasions? That can be a problem if the child senses friction between the parents. The issue is that the child may feel uncomfortable being affectionate and pleasant to both parents at the same time, especially in a public setting. In the worst scenario, the child may totally ignore the ''other parent'' or be very rude. The situation becomes uncomfortable for everybody. If that is the case, it might be best for the parents to agree to take turns attending these school events.

Teachers and school counselors have the opportunity to provide stability and self-respect to children of divorce, that they may sorely need. The children may find that their time at school is an island of tranquility compared to their home ports, which are very troubled. Although it is not the responsibility of school personnel to compensate for every child's serious family problems, teachers can be very helpful by being aware of the issue facing children of divorce and making small accommodations.

Chapter Thirteen
Mental Health Professionals

Ms. Sears had custody of her fourteen-year-old daughter, Sally, who had anorexia nervosa. There appeared to be an enmeshed relationship between mother and daughter, and both of them felt it was important for Sally to be as perfect a child as possible. The girl was in therapy with a child psychiatrist, who was also seeing the girl, the mother, and stepfather in family therapy.

The father, Mr. Roebuck, sought custody of Sally and the case went to court. The child psychiatrist agreed to testify and recommended that custody remain with Ms. Sears and the stepfather. The court upheld this recommendation. Since the child's therapist had said in court that the mother should be the custodial parent, Ms. Sears took the psychiatrist's testimony as unequivocal endorsement of her values and her parenting skills. Since she was doing such a good job, she decided to discontinue Sally's therapy. After all, a highly credentialed child psychiatrist had stated under oath that Ms. Sears was a good mother. The anorectic girl later required both medical and psychiatric hospitalizations, but the mother steadfastly maintained that her family had received the official stamp of approval.

In other words, the child's emotional condition worsened and her therapy was damaged because the therapist had agreed to testify regarding the custody dispute. She probably would have been better off if the therapist had stayed out of the dispute altogether.

Sally, Ms. Sears, and Mr. Roebuck will reappear later in this chapter.

Since about one-half of marriages in the United States end in divorce, there are many children and adolescents whose parents are separated, divorced, and perhaps remarried. Many of these children and their families have had the occasion to see mental health professionals for one reason or another. The purpose of this chapter is to explain the various roles that a mental health professional might have with the children of divorce. It is important to understand that these roles are quite distinct from each other. When a divorced parent starts seeing a mental health professional, it is important for both of them to clarify exactly what the parent is looking for and asking the therapist to do.

Defining the Therapist's Role

There are several ways in which a therapist might be involved with children of divorce and their family members.

● *As a therapist for the child.* The therapist may be seeing a youngster, whose parents are currently divorcing, or could be treating an adolescent, whose parents divorced many years earlier but whose emotional wounds are still tender. In the example at the beginning of the chapter, the psychiatrist was Sally Roebuck's therapist.

● *As a therapist for one of the parents.* Because the process of divorce creates such an emotional upheaval, many divorced parents find it helpful to have individual or group counseling.

● *As a family therapist.* The mental health professional may become the therapist for the new family that is created following the divorce. He may become the therapist for a blended family or some other complex combination of parents, stepparents, half-siblings, and stepsiblings. In the example, the psychiatrist was also the therapist for the Sears family.

● *As an expert witness* who has been asked to do a custody evaluation. In some custody disputes, one or both sides or the court itself arranges for the parents and the children to have a custody evaluation performed by a mental health professional, usually a psychologist or a psychiatrist. The purpose of the evaluation is to determine what custody arrangement is in the best interests of the children and to make recommendations to the court. In the example, the psychiatrist also became an expert witness, in addition to being a therapist.

● *As a divorce mediator.* A professional divorce mediator has studied both the psychological and the legal ramifications of divorce. It is his job to help the parties negotiate and agree on the property settlement and on custody and visitation arrangements. Divorce mediation is discussed in chapter fourteen.

• *As a counselor for the divorced parents.* The divorce counselor is a mental health professional who tries to help the parents find ways to raise their children in a cooperative manner. The basic mission of divorce counseling is to help parents avoid grinding the children up in the course of their own disputes. Divorce and visitation counseling is also discussed in chapter fourteen.

In the case of Sally Roebuck at the beginning of this chapter, the psychiatrist became involved in three different roles: as the therapist for Sally, the therapist for the family, and also as an expert witness at her custody trial. That was a mistake. The anecdote illustrates how important it is for the therapist to be extremely careful in keeping his role precisely defined. It is important for the therapist to not attempt to wear too many hats at once.

There are so many roles that mental health professionals may take, that a therapist's job may change as the divorce process moves forward and the family's needs change. The transition from one role to another does not always work. In some situations, in fact, the therapist should be absolutely clear that he cannot assume two different roles at the same time. It is very hard, for instance, for a psychiatrist who has already been functioning as the child's therapist to change hats and become an unbiased professional to perform a custody evaluation and to make recommendations to the court regarding custody and visitation. It would seem very hard, also, for one psychologist to be the individual therapist for two parents who are getting divorced from each other.

In other situations, a professional may be able to work with a client or a divorced family in more than one way. For instance, a psychologist might become involved with a divorcing family by doing a custody evaluation and during the evaluation, she would have the opportunity to meet and get to know both parents. Or she may have been a mediator who helped the parents negotiate an agreement regarding the property and the custody of the children. If both parents have come to respect and trust the same psychologist, the situation could evolve to where the psychologist becomes the divorce counselor and continues to help the divorced couple work out the details on an ongoing basis. It is also conceivable that after the evaluation is over and the legal issues are fully resolved, the psychologist who did the custody evaluation might become the therapist

Judith Wallerstein, Ph.D., and Joan B. Kelly designed a major longitudinal study of the responses of normal, psychologically healthy children and their parents to divorce. Their research was known as the California Children of Divorce Study. The children and their parents were interviewed at the time of marital separation, at eighteen months postseparation, at five years postseparation, and again at ten years following the separation of their parents. The original study was described by Wallerstein and Kelly in *Surviving the Breakup: How Children and Parents Cope with Divorce* (New York: Basic Books, 1980). The ten-year follow-up was described by Wallerstein and Blakeslee in *Second Chances: Men, Women, and Children a Decade after Divorce* (New York: Ticknor and Fields, 1989).

for one of the children. That would make particularly good sense if *both* parents still respected the psychologist's work.

Defining the Therapist's Mission

Any mental health professional who evaluates, treats, or counsels any member of a divorcing or divorced family should have a crystal-clear understanding of his role. After his role is defined, he also needs to clarify what his mission may be within that role. After agreeing on what the assignment is, somebody should say to the mental health professional, "That is your mission, if you choose to accept it." Basically, the therapist will do a better job if he knows what his client is expecting of him. This process of clarifying both the role and the mission is the joint responsibility of the mental health professional and the client. As a good consumer, the prospective client should be aware of exactly what he or she is asking the therapist to accomplish.

What exactly are the missions that a therapist may be asked to accomplish? In treating a child of divorced parents, for instance, the therapist may be expected to help the child be more happy, less worried, better behaved, and more successful in school. In most divorced families, it should be understood that the purpose of the therapy is to help the child love and respect both his parents. Usually it is up to the therapist to clarify this point, that the purpose of the counseling is to help the child have a happy and comfortable and satisfying relationship with both parents. It may be important for the therapist and both parents to discuss this subject explicitly at the beginning.

In some divorced families, the purpose of the child's therapy may not be to help the child have a satisfying relationship with both parents. In fact, the purpose of the therapy may be just the opposite. For instance, it may be that the child's noncustodial parent has withdrawn from the relationship, has no interest in keeping in touch, and it is unlikely that he or she will ever change. In such a situation, the therapist may need to help the child accept that the noncustodial parent is not going to match up to the child's fantasies. Sometimes children have extremely elaborate wishful fantasies about the whereabouts and careers and intentions of the parents who have abandoned them.

Signals of Emotional Distress

Children react to the stress of parental divorce in many ways. If the youngster is having serious symptoms, he may need evaluation by a mental health professional. In some cases the counselor may be able to help the child through a crisis by having only two or three meetings. In conducting the evaluation, the counselor may ask the parent about symptoms like these:

● *Worrying too much.* A child's emotional distress may be manifested by continuing anxiety, fearfulness, and related symptoms, such as repetitive nightmares.

● *Not worrying enough.* Some children distance themselves from family events and family conflict and act as though they are not involved in or bothered by these issues. To some extent, this kind of defense mechanism may be adaptive and useful for the child. However, if the child totally denies any interest in or concern about serious events in the family, it may mean that he is not dealing with his feelings in a healthy way.

● *Depression.* This is the most common response to divorce and other serious family problems. The child may be apathetic, tearful, and obviously unhappy. His depression may be more subtle. For instance, it may be manifested by withdrawal from family social events and a lack of interest in activities that would ordinarily be considered fun.

• *Physical symptoms.* Sometimes stomachaches, headaches, and more dramatic symptoms, such as fainting spells, may be the sign of emotional problems in a child or adolescent.

• *Oppositional and disruptive behaviors.* When a child who is usually pleasant and compliant is put under stress, especially stress related to family conflict, the youngster may become argumentative and oppositional. Sometimes children manifest their emotional distress by delinquent behavior such as fighting, stealing, and breaking rules.

• *Deterioration in the child's usual level of functioning.* This deterioration may mean the loss of a developmental skill that has already been achieved, such as fecal soiling by a young child who had already been toilet trained. It could mean very poor school grades by a youngster who previously had been a good student.

Implications for Psychotherapy

When helping the child or adolescent deal with parental divorce, the therapist may find it helpful to be more directive than usual. For instance, the youngster may find himself being sucked into the parental conflict. He may find himself actively allying himself with one parent and rejecting the other. He may feel it is his job to negotiate both big and little issues between the parents. Since the divorce makes his parents miserable, he may think it is up to him to make them happy. It is usually good to advise the child to stay out of the fighting and to try to be reasonably neutral. That may be hard to do since the parents may be campaigning for the youngster's vote and affection.

Therapists may see youngsters whose parents divorced many years earlier and who are now referred for a completely separate reason. In such a case, an adolescent may appear open and nondefensive about the details and the circumstances of his parents' divorce. He is likely to say some form of: "It really doesn't bother me . . . it was a long time ago . . . it doesn't matter anyway, since there's nothing I can do about it. . . ." The therapist who pursues this matter patiently will probably find that the divorce really does matter in many ways. The youngster is likely to feel resentment that most of his childhood and adolescence has been affected by his parents' needs and preferences. He has repeatedly had to accommodate his schedule to theirs, to move from one household and community to another, to maintain a fragile relationship with the noncustodial parent through visitation, to adapt to stepparents, to give up the closeness and simplicity of an intact nuclear family, and so on.

You Need Two Heads to Wear Two Hats

The most common dilemma for therapists in the context of a custody dispute is to be asked to take on two conflicting roles at the same time. One role is that the psychiatrist or social worker or psychologist has been asked to perform an independent custody evaluation. Such an evaluation usually consists of an assessment of the youngster and of both parents and recommendations that are intended to be in the best interests of the child. The second possible role is that the professional has already been involved as the therapist of the child or of one of the parents. In these situations a professional may choose *either* to be the evaluator *or* to be the therapist, but it rarely works to try to do both at the same time. When a new client is referred for evaluation, it is helpful to clarify from the outset whether one's role is to conduct an evaluation for the use of the court or to conduct a clinical evaluation and provide therapy.

It is not unusual to already be treating a child or an adolescent at the point where the parents embark on a full-fledged custody dispute. It almost always happens that the custodial parent, who was the parent who brought the youngster for therapy in the first place, and the custodial parent's attorney ask the therapist to become actively involved in the custody dispute. That usually means for the therapist to write a report that recommends that the patient stay with the custodial parent and perhaps testify at a deposition or at court. All of this raises the question: What should be the role of the child's therapist when one of the parents has initiated a custody dispute and the court is intending to determine the patient's placement? It is my opinion that a therapist who is already involved in a therapeutic relationship should emphasize his role of helping the patient express his feelings, explore his fantasies, and deal with the events that are occurring in his life. In most situations it will be preferable for the therapist to emphasize the importance of his work with the child and to decline the invitation to become actively involved in the custody dispute. That is, the therapist should confine himself to helping the patient deal with the process and outcome of the custody dispute and should not try to influence the outcome of the dispute by sending written reports and testifying.

The custodial parent and the attorney usually feel very strongly that the therapist is the ideal person to testify, since the therapist has come to understand the child patient so well and since the therapist can be considered an expert in these matters. The therapist should take care not to succumb to the flattery. Although it looks superficially like the child's therapist is the perfect person to testify in a custody dispute, he really is not a good choice at all. For one thing, the therapist is almost certainly biased in favor of the custodial parent, even though he may try very hard to feel neutral. His biases make his testimony almost worthless. Furthermore, there are risks involved in testifying. For instance, the confidential nature of the therapy will almost certainly be violated if the therapist testifies. Also, the therapist's testimony may adversely affect any future therapy with his client. The therapist's active role in influencing the outcome of the custody dispute is going to change the therapeutic alliance with the patient and will also change the relationship with the patient's parents.

Even when the therapist's opinion is adopted by the court, the effect on the therapy itself can be damaging. That phenomenon was illustrated in the example at the beginning of this chapter, the case of Ms. Sears and Mr. Roebuck. In that case the psychiatrist was trying to be helpful, but his testimony was misinterpreted by the custodial parent, Ms. Sears. Since the doctor went to court and testified on behalf of Sally and Ms. Sears, they took that to mean that Sally didn't have any more problems and they ended her therapy. Her condition worsened and she had to be hospitalized.

Although it is usually best for the therapist to avoid active participation in these disputes, the therapist may wish to become involved indirectly by sharing verbal information with the independent mental health professional who is performing the custody evaluation. When the therapist is invited by a parent, an attorney, or a judge to participate actively and make recommendations regarding custody, the therapist can use the opportunity to explain the possible disadvantages of his taking that role. For instance, the attorney will probably have a better case if an independent psychiatrist supports his position rather than the potentially biased therapist.

The Basic Message

The most important thing for divorced parents and mental health professionals to remember is to be clear with each other regarding assumptions and expectations. If a parent really has in mind that the therapist is going to testify on his or her behalf in court in two months, the parent needs to say so at the beginning. If the therapist is working on the assumption that the confidentiality of the child's therapy is going to be protected from future legal proceedings, he needs to say so at the beginning.

Taking your child to a therapist is like taking your car to a garage. If you want the mechanic to check the brakes, you need to spell it out and make it clear what you are expecting. Then the mechanic can tell you whether he works on brakes. Likewise, the parent and the therapist need to be very clear with each other regarding what they see is the purpose of the therapy.

Chapter Fourteen
Divorce Mediation

Cynthia Ryback and Howard Ryback had been married for ten years. By the time they decided to divorce, they both had plenty of ammunition and could have waged a substantial battle over custody of their two children, a five-year-old girl and a seven-year-old boy. Cynthia was ready to allege that Howard had been alcoholic and had hit her and the children when he was intoxicated. Howard had hired a private investigator, who was ready to testify that Cynthia had stayed overnight with a male friend, when she said she was visiting her sister. Both of the parents worked, although the father, a supervisor in a laboratory, had a considerably higher income than the mother, who taught junior high school. They both felt very aggrieved and very resentful. They had hired attorneys and were trying to get the money together for a prolonged court trial, because they both were seeking custody of the children.

Cynthia's sister had heard about divorce mediation and told Cynthia what it was. She told Cynthia that going to trial would be extremely expensive, would be very upsetting, and might be damaging for the children. Cynthia was concerned that she might not get the outcome she wanted through mediation, but she decided to call a mediator and get more information. The mediator was an attorney, who initially met with both parents at the same time. He also met with them individually, to help the parents define what they really wanted for themselves during and after the divorce. The mediator was knowledgeable about estate planning and taxes and was able to make some suggestions that saved Cynthia and Howard a good deal of money.

It became clear during the mediation process that Howard was at a critical point in his career and he was very interested in working hard in order to achieve a promotion. He really did not want to have the everyday responsibility for the children, but he wanted to be with them regularly and he wanted assurances that the mother was not going to take the children and move to another community. Since the mother was a teacher, she was much more available to supervise the children, especially during school vacations. They ultimately agreed on joint custody, with the children primarily living with the mother. They worked out a plan for how to handle the children's education, medical care, and religious upbringing. Since the father had a higher income, he agreed to a reasonable amount of child support. Since the mother was working and she was allowed to remain in the family home, there was no alimony. She agreed to pay the mortgage. The mediator helped Cynthia and Howard agree to a formula for how the money would be distributed when the house was later sold.

The mediator was no magician, but he simply worked with the parents until there was a plan that both parties could live with. In order to make sure that their rights were being protected, both parents took a draft of the proposal to their respective attorneys, who made some minor suggestions. They presented the final version to the judge, and Cynthia and Howard ended up with a relatively nontraumatic divorce.

Mediation Is Not Therapy

Divorce mediation is a form of negotiation in which a trained individual, the mediator, helps two individuals who are divorcing work out the division of the marital property, the custody of the children, and all the other details related to the divorce. The purpose of divorce mediation is not to help the parents improve their relationship and get back together again. The purpose of divorce mediation is to help the parents achieve a relatively nonadversarial divorce. It is also intended to help the parents negotiate the arrangements for the children, including everything from schooling to bedtimes. In some states (such as California, Maine, New Mexico, Oregon, and Wisconsin), an attempt at mediation is required before a divorce is granted.

Mediation is not the same as marriage counseling. In marriage counseling, the counselor is trying to help the couple communicate and have a better relationship. In divorce mediation, it is understood by everybody that the marriage is over and the purpose of the meetings is to work out the terms of the divorce. Divorce mediation is not the same as arbitration. In arbitration the ground rules usually provide that the neutral arbitrator

There is a long discussion of divorce mediation in the new edition of a book by Richard Gardner, *The Parents' Book About Divorce* (New York: Bantam Books, 1991). For mental health professionals, there are several good books regarding this subject, including: *Child Custody Mediation* by F. Bienenfeld (Science and Behavior Books, 1983) and *The Handbook of Divorce Mediation* by S. Marlow and S. R. Sauber (New York: Plenum Press, 1990). Another book on this topic is by a married couple, John Haynes and Gretchen Haynes, who wrote *Mediating Divorce: A Casebook of Strategies for Successful Family Negotiations* (San Francisco: Jossey-Bass, 1989). There is a chapter on this subject in *Emerging Issues in Child Psychiatry and the Law,* which was edited by D. H. Schetky and E. P. Benedek (New York: Brunner/Mazel, 1985).

will make the final decision regarding the dispute. In mediation, the neutral mediator does not make the final decision, but helps the divorcing couple arrive at a mutual agreement. Divorce mediation is a way for parents to communicate their needs to each other and to work out their disagreements.

Mediation is facilitated by a neutral individual, who may be an attorney (who has additional training in psychological processes) or a mental health professional (who has additional training in legal issues). Divorce is a complicated process. If the mediator is an attorney, it may be necessary to use a psychiatrist or a psychologist to help the parents understand the needs of the children. If the parents cannot agree on the custody of the children, the mediator may suggest that they arrange for a neutral psychiatrist or psychologist to conduct a formal custody evaluation. The recommendation of the mental health professional would then be fed into the mediation process. On the other hand, if the mediator is a mental health professional, it may be necessary to consult with an attorney if there are unusually complicated legal questions, such as the tax implications of the division of the marital property.

Mediation is a good idea for divorcing couples who would rather save their money for the children's college education than spend it all in a four-day court battle. For mediation to work, both parents have to be open minded enough to negotiate in a sincere manner. It is also necessary for each parent to have some respect for the point of view and the desires of the other parent, even though they may still be quite angry at each other. Finally, it is necessary for each parent to be reasonably trustworthy. The process will not work if one parent has assets that are hidden from the purview of the other party.

Even if an attorney is the mediator, almost always the divorcing individuals still have their own attorneys. That may become important in order to protect the interests of the individual parents. Once the mediation is over, each party should ask his or her attorney to review the agreement. Occasionally the attorneys pick up something that seems unreasonable or unfair, that had escaped the notice of their clients.

Parenting Plan

Another way to reduce the amount of fighting over the children and through the children is to develop a formal parenting plan. Some states, such as Washington, require the presentation of a parenting plan when a couple seeks a divorce. The parenting plan is a detailed document that specifies all the issues regarding the children ahead of time, so it is less likely that arguments will occur later. The parenting plan would address the schedule the child has at each household; the plan for the child's education, including the name of the school and who is going to pay for it; the plan for medical care, including the name of the pediatrician and who is able to authorize medical care; the plan for religious training, such as which parent is going to take the child to church and to Sunday school; and anything else that either parent might want to clarify. Most divorcing parents would need some help in developing a parenting plan. In some cases the parents' two attorneys would help them work out the details. In other cases, the parents might need the assistance of a divorce mediator.

Counseling for Divorced Parents

Divorce counseling refers to meetings that divorced parents have with a mental health professional. For instance, the therapist may meet with the divorced parents together on a regular basis, such as once a month. I am not talking about meetings that take place prior to the divorce, as happens in divorce mediation, but meetings that take place after the divorce is over and the parents are starting to lead their separate lives. The purpose of these meetings is to discuss how the two divorced parents

100

can raise their children in a cooperative and reasonable manner. The most important aspect of this kind of counseling is simply establishing good communication between the parents. For instance, the therapist would be the moderator for discussions on topics such as: clarifying exactly what the visitation schedule is going to be over Thanksgiving vacation this year; figuring out how the youngster can be on his high-school basketball team when he is living in two households; and comparing plans for birthday presents, so that both parents do not give the son exactly the same ten-speed bicycle.

In working with divorced parents, it is necessary for the therapist to structure the meetings and keep the parents on task. That is, it does not do anybody much good if the meeting degenerates into a session for digging up old grievances and for angry backbiting. Divorce counseling is not the same as psychotherapy for the parents. It is simply a way to help the parents communicate and resolve issues rather than perpetuate the disagreements.

Sometimes the counselor who is working with divorced parents may want to see the children. For instance, suppose there is a great deal of conflict related to the visitations. The parents argue endlessly about the fact that the father picks the children up at the wrong time; exposes them to the unsavory relatives in his extended family; fails to get them to soccer practice, as he had agreed to; and brings the children back dirty and hungry. The visitation happens every other weekend, so the therapist arranges a schedule for a meeting to occur once a week. During the week after the visitation, the therapist meets with the children as a group. They discuss how the last visitation went, what was good, what was bad, what was fun, and what they might prefer to do differently. They discuss some possible plans for the next visitation.

During the next week, the therapist has a meeting with the two parents. After comparing notes about what happened during the previous visitation, they have a very specific discussion about the plans for the upcoming visitation. They clarify very precisely what the schedule will be and what the various activities will be for the children. After that the visitation occurs; then the meeting with the children; then the meeting with the parents; and so on. The purpose of this form of counseling is not for the custodial parent to control what happens during the children's time with the noncustodial parent. The purpose is to have clear communication, with the ultimate goal being that the children will have a good relationship with both parents. This kind of counseling helps the children have a healthy and meaningful relationship with the noncustodial parent.

Therapists work with divorced families in many different ways—before, during, and after the divorce. In order to be good consumers, the parents should be clear about what they want from their therapists. Depending on the circumstances, the therapist may work primarily with the parents or primarily with the children. The mental health professional's role may be to do therapy, or to mediate, or to do an evaluation for court. At times, therapists should be clever and creative in thinking out a treatment plan. Above all, they need to be very clear about what their job is in each individual case. It is not possible to be everything for everybody.

Chapter Fifteen
Letting Go and Moving On

David and Jessica Trucker separated several times during their short but tumultuous marriage. When they were apart, they missed each other. When they were together, they disagreed on practically everything. They eventually divorced, but afterwards David and Jessica continued to see each other. When Jessica's garbage disposal stopped working, David came over and fixed it. When David was lonely, Jessica went to his apartment, where they fixed dinner and sometimes had sex together.

David became depressed and his performance at work deteriorated to the point where he sought help from his employee assistance program. The EAP counselor, a woman, met with David three times. He was very open with her and shared both his memories and his feelings. In fact, he seemed to become overly attached to and dependent on the counselor. For example, he gave the therapist a small present. And he had a few "anxiety attacks," when he phoned the therapist's office and answering service, in order to hear her reassuring voice. When he couldn't reach the therapist, David continued to call Jessica for support.

The therapist told David that he needed to move on with his life. In particular, he and his former wife needed to be less dependent emotionally on each other: Jessica should find somebody else to fix her plumbing; David should find other people to hang around with. David decided to talk this over with a couple of men he knew at work, who were also divorced. The three men had similar experiences in their marriages and also in their divorces and found it helpful to compare their experiences. As time went on, David stopped worrying about Jessica's garbage disposal and he was no longer anxious and depressed.

This sounds like a simple story, but it was hard for David to think of himself as a divorced guy rather than a married guy. Once he did, he was able to let go of his relationship with Jessica and move on.

Sometimes it seems puzzling that two people who can't stand each other still stay involved in each other's lives. Of course, it is understandable because intense interpersonal relationships are more complicated than simply "liking" or "not liking" somebody. Frequently people have intense, but ambivalent, relationships. That is, David probably felt very attached to Jessica and very positive about some aspects of her personality and mind and body. He presumably disliked or felt very negative about other parts of Jessica. Likewise Jessica may have had strong ambivalent feelings about David.

I think that ambivalent relationships continue to tie people together even after they separate and divorce. This is one reason why some people have difficulty leaving a former spouse alone: they continue to be emotionally enmeshed, even though they know the relationship is destructive.

Having the Last Word

There are other reasons why divorced individuals continue to contact each other and pester each other. For example, feeling hurt and angry and wanting revenge. Getting divorced is a very hurtful experience in many ways. Perhaps the most important way is that getting divorced is like being told that you have been a failure for all those years, that a big chunk of your life has been a waste of time. Getting divorced is a serious blow to a person's pride or his narcissism.

The other big reason for anger is that one partner has taken steps to terminate the marriage, so the other person feels wounded and enraged. It may be that both parties have reason to feel abandoned and rejected, so they both are enraged at each other. Of course, once the divorce gets going, people do a lot of mean things to each other, so there is even more reason to stay angry and to keep the arguing going. Both parties want to have the last word, usually in a very big way.

What to Do About It

There are many suggestions that might be offered to people who find themselves in this situation, who need to leave behind old relationships and move on with their lives. This chapter contains some specific suggestions, but I'm sure that anybody who has been through a difficult divorce can add to this list.

- Deal with the feelings that you are experiencing, instead of denying them or burying them. That means: talk it out with family and close friends; cry a lot, at least for a while; get angry and call a few names.
- Find people who are in the same boat. You probably know them already, but never thought of them as people to socialize with because they were divorced and you were married. Now that you are single again, you will probably enjoy spending some time with people who have had similar experiences. These people will probably become part of your personal support network.
- There is a chapter of Parents Without Partners in many cities. Call them up.
- Renew contact with your parents and siblings. That is not to say that you should go home to Mom and Dad and just sit there for the next three years, but you will probably enjoy being included on holidays and other special occasions.
- There are more formal ways of getting through rough times. Many churches and other community agencies have both support groups and organized social activities for divorced individuals. It might seem hard to make the initial contact with such a group, but I'm sure they will try to include you and help you feel comfortable.
- If you have children, there is even more reason why you need a support network. It is very hard to raise children all by yourself. Single parents get tired of watching ''Barney'' every day. Watching dinosaurs sing songs can get old if you don't get a break from it every so often. Single parents need the company of other adults at times, in order to have conversations about grown-up subjects.
- Focus on your plans for this week, for next week, and for the next couple of months. Don't dwell on the past more than you have to.
- See if you can frame your divorce in the most positive way you can think of. That usually takes the form of something like this: ''I'm glad that I finally got rid of that bum, so that now I can look after myself instead of catering to him all the time.''

Don't Do This

It should be clear to readers of this book that prolonged angry relationships between divorced parents are not good for the children. It is in

Judith Viorst is a prolific writer and a thoughtful person. Her work has ranged from children's books (*Alexander and the Terrible, Horrible, No Good, Very Bad Day*) to books about human nature and human development (*How Did I Get to Be Forty and Other Atrocities*). In *Necessary Losses* (New York: Simon & Schuster, 1986), Ms. Viorst merged her personal experiences as a daughter and mother and wife with her training as a research graduate of the Washington Psychoanalytic Institute. She emphasized that there are many, many losses and disappointments which we all encounter during every stage of life. Her point was that "these losses are a part of life—universal, unavoidable, inexorable. And these losses are necessary because we grow by losing and leaving and letting go." Ms. Viorst's message is particularly important for divorcing parents and their children.

Another book that discusses how to let go after divorce is *Uncoupling: Turning Points in Intimate Relationships* (New York: Oxford University Press, 1986), by Diane Vaughn.

your interests and also in the children's interests to call it quits, to leave that relationship behind, and to move on with your life. What makes it complicated is that the prospect of raising children together automatically means that the divorced parents are going to stay in touch and communicate with each other. Since divorced parents cannot usually wave goodbye and move to another state, it is necessary to create a relationship that is civil, rather businesslike, and constructive from the point of view of the children. The best way to define such a relationship is to give some examples of activities that do not seem to make sense or to be helpful to anybody and later to give other examples of behaviors that seem constructive.

• Don't rely on each other for all the little things that you used to rely on each other for. Find somebody else to tune up your car, to cut your hair, to do your income tax.

• When the noncustodial parent has the child for visitation, he should not rely on the custodial parent to solve minor problems. If the child has a headache, for example, he should try to figure out for himself how many baby aspirins to give.

- Don't start dating your former spouse or have sexual activities together. I suppose there are exceptions to this and to every other rule in life, since occasionally divorced individuals decide to get married again, but this rule certainly seems like a good policy to follow most of the time.
- Don't entertain the idea that it would be good to organize a nice happy Christmas together, with both of the parents and both sets of grandparents all enjoying each other's company. Once again, I guess there are exceptions because I have heard of families who are able to make this happen. Most divorced families, however, should not try to re-create the good old days, which is supposedly being done for the sake of the children.
- Likewise, I suggest that you don't try to spend a week at the beach with your ex-spouse and your kids.
- Don't spend your energy and your financial resources on legal battles, any more than you need to in order to protect your legitimate interests. That means that you should not go back to court over and over if your only real purpose there is to get revenge or to show that you can have the last word by winning on some minor issue.

Do This

There are many times when divorced parents will need to communicate and collaborate. Some examples may help define the difference between constructive communication and beating a dead relationship.

- One of the themes of this book has been that divorced parents need to communicate about many aspects of child rearing. On some items they need to reach agreement, such as the exact times of the visitation schedule. On many other items, they may not reach agreement, but they should at least listen to each other regarding topics such as the child's education, medical care, and household rules.
- When there is conflict between parents, I have suggested that some aspects of the child rearing should be done independently, in order to reduce the fighting. For example, suppose that both parents like to help their fourteen-year-old daughter, Nancy, with schoolwork, but they give conflicting advice. Nancy gets frustrated and angry when she is caught between these well-meaning parents. So the parents agree to divide their efforts: the mother will help Nancy with her science fair project and leave

the algebra alone; the father will go over Nancy's algebra homework, but will refrain from making suggestions about the science fair.

• There are occasions when divorced parents should make a strong effort to lay aside animosity, at least temporarily. Think about those important, singular times when children should feel proud of themselves and should feel good about their families—an example would be high school graduation. It seems to me that is one time that divorced parents should be able to be in the same room at the same time. They are likely to have approximately the same thought: "It's great that Johnny has made it to this point in his life."

• Moving ahead a few years, what about the child's wedding? Ann Landers must get hundreds or thousands of letters about this topic. When the parents get divorced, who should be invited to the wedding? Who should be excluded? Who should give away the bride, the father or the stepfather? Who should help pick out the silver pattern, the mother or the stepmother? I realize there are no simple answers to these questions. If there were, Ann Landers would simply write them all down and everybody could follow them. However, I do think that a good general rule for weddings is for the divorced parents to put aside the mutual bitterness, that probably started years previously, and to create a beautiful day.

• There may be other times when a divorced person should enter into the affairs of his or her former spouse, that go against the general rule of staying out of each other's hair. Suppose, for example, that one of the parents has suffered an unusual crisis. Once there was a mother who found that she had a serious form of leukemia. Although she and her ex-husband had waged several serious battles, especially over their children, the father sincerely wanted to be helpful. The father was a medical administrator and was able to locate a cancer research group that offered the mother specialized treatment. The man became rather involved with his former spouse's illness, but it seemed like the right thing to do.

"Letting go and moving on" can be a painful process, but it is part of many life experiences that we all have had. This chapter is an echo of the three basic principles that were stated at the beginning of this book: that children of divorce should have a good relationship with both parents; that divorced parents should find ways to minimize the disruptions and make life as normal as possible for their children; and that divorced parents and their children need to accept the inevitable losses and disappointments and to move on with their lives. Let us hope that divorced parents and their children will be able to put their troubles into perspective and will be able to focus their energies on creating a brighter future rather than on reliving the past.

Chapter Sixteen
Ten Steps

Wc live in a complex world, and there are no quick and easy answers for most problems in our society. That goes for raising children of divorced parents. Since life is complex, it is good to stay on the main road with the central issues and not get sidetracked into petty and peripheral areas. Here are my suggestions for the most important things to remember about raising children of divorce.

Ten Steps for Raising Children in Divorced Families

1. Don't fight over the children, through the children, or in front of the children.
2. Children need to love and respect both parents.
3. Find ways to help the children have two homes, rather than one home and one hotel room.
4. Give appropriate consideration to the children's wishes.
5. Despite the divorce, find ways to create enduring family traditions.
6. Recognize the rights of both the custodial and the noncustodial parents.
7. Both children and parents should develop and maintain interests that go beyond the divorce.
8. Both children and parents should move on with their lives. They should accept the fact that life may not be exactly the way they would have planned it.
9. Don't try to do it by yourself—reach out and seek support from family, friends, and support groups.
10. When you need extra help, make use of professionals, such as clergy and therapists.